Daniel McAlpine, Archibald N. McAlpine

Biological Atlas

A guide to the practical study of plants and animals; adapted to the

requirements of the London university, science and art department, and

for use in schools and colleges

Daniel McAlpine, Archibald N. McAlpine

Biological Atlas
*A guide to the practical study of plants and animals; adapted to the requirements
of the London university, science and art department, and for use in schools and
colleges*

ISBN/EAN: 9783337105235

Printed in Europe, USA, Canada, Australia, Japan

Cover: Foto ©Andreas Hilbeck / pixelio.de

More available books at **www.hansebooks.com**

BIOLOGICAL ATLAS

A GUIDE TO THE PRACTICAL STUDY OF PLANTS AND ANIMALS

Adapted to the requirements of the London University, Science and Art Department, and for use in Schools and Colleges

WITH ACCOMPANYING TEXT

CONTAINING

ARRANGEMENT AND EXPLANATION, EQUIVALENT TERMS, GLOSSARY AND CLASSIFICATION

423 COLOURED FIGURES AND DIAGRAMS

BY

D. M'ALPINE, F.C.S.

LECTURER ON BIOLOGY AND BOTANY, EDINBURGH, AND DEMONSTRATOR OF THE SCIENCE AND ART DEPARTMENT; AUTHOR OF "FIRST NOTES FOR BIOLOGICAL STUDENTS," AND "A ZOOLOGICAL ATLAS"

AND

A. N. M'ALPINE, B.Sc. (Honours) Lond.

LECTURER ON BOTANY, SCHOOL OF MEDICINE, EDINBURGH; PROFESSOR OF BOTANY AND NATURAL HISTORY, NEW VETERINARY COLLEGE, EDINBURGH, AND ASSOCIATE OF THE ROYAL COLLEGE OF SCIENCE FOR IRELAND

FIFTH THOUSAND

W. & A. K. JOHNSTON
EDINBURGH AND LONDON
MDCCCLXXXI

PREFACE.

It is now generally recognised that a certain acquaintance with actual specimens is necessary for the proper understanding of Plants and Animals. By the practical study of representative forms, exemplifying the leading modifications of plant and animal life, the student obtains a basis of distinctly observed fact with which to compare other forms, and round which to cluster the information derived from books.

The University of London has given practical shape to this idea by selecting a series of common types which "each candidate must be prepared to examine microscopically, to dissect and to describe."

In this Atlas, which is intended to serve as a guide to, and not as a substitute for, practical work, drawings are given of the various points of importance exemplified by each of these types, to enable the student to make out the points for himself on the actual specimens. Experience both as students and teachers has taught us, that in this constant appeal to the object itself, the student is greatly assisted by clear and accurate drawings. In the triple alliance, as it may be called, of description, drawing, and object, is found the easiest, safest, and surest means of successful study.

Not only is the Atlas a guide to practical work, but since it contains the results of that work in a permanent form, a glance at the drawings with their accompanying description will serve as a valuable refresher to the memory before going up for examination.

Further, the Atlas may be used with any of the Text-books of Zoology or Botany in common use, such as those of Huxley, Nicholson, Macalister, Sachs, M'Nab, etc., because equivalent terms are noted in the text, and thus the language of the science is translated as it were into the different dialects.

The drawings belonging to each form represent the leading features in the history of its life. The structure as a whole is first shown, then the details of the various parts by means of separate drawings, and finally so much of the history of its development as is likely to be required.

In every case the types represented have been practically examined, and drawings made from nature. A number of the drawings are taken from dissections and microscopic preparations made in the Biological Laboratory of the Royal School of Mines, London. Others are copied from reliable sources whenever they give clearly and correctly the most instructive view of the object. In the development special care has been taken to give only such representations as were drawn by practised observers, e.g. the development of the Amœba is taken from Haeckel, and that of the Crayfish from Rathke.

Drawings after nature are headed Figures, and Diagrams are occasionally introduced for explanatory purposes.

The explanatory text *arranges* the information obtained from the drawing in a convenient form, *explains* briefly the nature of the object seen, states *equivalent terms* when the same thing is differently named by standard authors, gives the *derivation* of names when that throws light on their meaning, and *marks them* when there is any danger of wrong pronunciation, and finally sums up the *distinctive characters* in the form of a *classification*.

A few general practical directions are given to enable the student to adopt those expedients in the examination of specimens which experience has shown to be the best. These instructions are necessarily brief, but a detailed account is less necessary since the methods to be pursued are given clearly and at length in Huxley and Martin's Elementary Biology, to which the student is referred.

The following features of the Atlas may be specially mentioned:—

The names of the various parts are placed on the drawing.

The description faces the Plate.

Colour is used to distinguish the different organs, and as a rule, corresponding parts have the same colour throughout in order to render comparison easy.

The size of a microscopic object is generally given, or shown by means of squares, to prevent misconception.

The comparative Histology of Frog and Man shows that a close correspondence exists between the structure of the Frog and that of higher animals, and thus justifies its detailed study as a representative form.

The complete life-history is usually given.

Separate drawings are freely used for the different systems of the Plant or Animal body, and thus all the evils and confusion arising from overcrowding are prevented.

Equivalent terms allow of its being used with any standard text-book.

No apology is needed for issuing a work of this kind. While there are large and well-executed wall-diagrams which the student may admire at a distance, there is no set of drawings at a convenient price and in a handy form which he can use as a map to show him the various regions of the Plant or Animal, and guide him in his attempts to explore them. It is hoped that the cheap and convenient form of the Atlas may favour its introduction even into higher-class schools. There the study of Biology might be made a powerful instrument, both of information and training, and a valuable preliminary to the study of Physiology.

We are much indebted to Mr. S. P. Eastick for valuable aid received while the work was in progress. No pains have been spared to ensure accuracy, yet doubtless some mistakes have escaped notice.

EDINBURGH, *January* 1880.

PREFACE TO THE SECOND EDITION.

The attempt to encourage practical work in Biology by means of clear figures briefly explained, and accompanied by instructions for the examination of specimens, has evidently been received with favour, since a second edition of the "Biological Atlas" has been called for within a year of publication.

Both Text and Plates have been carefully revised, and such alterations and improvements made as will tend to render it still more serviceable. However, few changes have been found necessary.

The colouring of the Animal portion of the work has been somewhat altered, in order to bring it into harmony with that of the "Zoological Atlas," to which the present work may be regarded as an introduction.

D. M'A.

Edinburgh, *April* 1884.

LIST OF PLATES.

GENERAL DIRECTIONS FOR PRACTICAL WORK.

For the examination and dissection of the various specimens the following apparatus will be required :—

Dissecting Instruments.—Sharp knife or scalpel; forceps; dissecting needles; scissors; and dissecting dish.

Dissecting needles may be readily made by fastening ordinary needles in penholders. To fasten the needle, hold it in a pair of pliers and push the sharp end into the wood; withdraw the needle again and insert the blunt end. These needles may be made to cut by grinding edges on them. The needle is readily bent by heating in a gas flame and bending with the pliers. Such needles are very useful in dissecting flowers.

Dissecting Dish.—A shallow vessel may be used, with a plate of wax, gutta-percha, or black paraffin (prepared by melting down solid paraffin and lampblack) covering the bottom, on which to cut up or pin down the specimen. A tight-fitting lid with a layer of cork fastened to the inside can be used as a dissecting board.

Optical Instruments.—Microscope; pocket lens, which may be used also as a dissecting microscope by having a fixed rod on which it can be moved up or down, leaving the hands free for teasing, etc.; watch-maker's magnifying-glass, which may be used in dissecting out nerves, blood-vessels, or any minute structures.

Small apertures are best made out by taking a glass tube drawn out to a fine point and blowing through it to enlarge the opening. Bristles can then be readily inserted.

Reagents, &c.—Distilled water; weak spirit; solutions of magenta, carmine, iodine, salt, potash, and chromic acid; glycerine; acetic acid.

A weak solution of bichromate of potash may be used instead of spirit for preserving.

A good plan for dropping reagents is to fix glass rods in the corks of the bottles.

YEAST.

Mounting.—Get some Yeast at the brewer's or the baker's, and place a small drop on a glass slide. Cover with a cover-glass for examination under a high power of the microscope.

Staining.—Place a little of the staining solution beside the cover-glass, and arrange a slip of blotting-paper at the opposite side, so as to cause a current of the staining material.

Crushing.—By gentle pressure of the finger or some blunt instrument the wall will burst and the contents flow out. To prevent breaking and damming of the cover-glass it is protected by a tiny pad of blotting-paper.

BACTERIA.

Mince some lean meat and soak in cold water for an hour; filter, and keep in a warm place for several days; examine the liquid and the scum which forms on the surface with the highest power of the microscope.

MOULDS.

Teasing.—Take a very small portion of the mould and lay it on a slide with a little water, then tease out by means of two dissecting needles.

PROTOCOCCUS.

Mounting.—Take a bit of the bark of any tree with green scum upon it, brush off the Protococci and mount in water.

Mount a drop of water from a water-butt containing Protococci, stain with iodine, which kills the Protococci and renders the cilia visible.

CHARA.

Hardening.—A weak solution of chromic acid is used. The chromic acid, in addition to its hardening action, acts also as a solvent, dissolving any limy incrustation.

Embedding the slender Stem.—Soak a piece with gum, which will fill up any cavities; then harden the gum by dipping in alcohol, which removes water, leaving the stem surrounded by a coat of hardened gum. Place a little bit thus prepared in a hole scooped out in solid paraffin. Melt a little paraffin in a small spoon and pour around the specimen.

Section-cutting.—Wet razor with alcohol by means of a brush. Cut a number of slices and transfer them with the brush to a watch-glass. Add water, the gum dissolves, and the sections become detached from the paraffin.

FERN.

Sections.—The rhizome cuts better after steeping for some time.

Staining.—A transverse section of fibro-vascular bundle, for instance, consisting of hard and close-set cells, may be stained by soaking with magenta for some time in a watch-glass, then washing with water from a pipette before mounting.

FLOWERING PLANT.

Leaf.—Cut a small piece out of blade of leaf. Dip it into gum and then into alcohol. Imbed in paraffin and cut transverse sections.

Peel off a small bit of epidermis from the lower surface, say, of a geranium leaf, and examine in water.

Anther.—Take anther from a flower before it opens. Dip in gum and alcohol before imbedding and cutting sections.

Ovule.—One of the Speedwells may be used, *e.g.* Buxbaum's Speedwell. Dissect out ovules from ovary of flower from which corolla has just fallen, then tease them asunder under dissecting microscope in a drop of potash solution and add a little glycerine when mounting.

Embryo.—The common Shepherd's Purse may be used. Dissect out the mature ovules or seeds from fruit. Commence with youngest fruit nearest the top, afterwards going to older, to get different stages. Mount in potash solution, press gently with coverglass, and the embryo will be forced out through the micropyle.

Seeds.—Beans or Peas are readily examined after steeping for a night in water.

Germination.—Wheat and Indian Corn can be readily germinated by placing in moist tow, surrounded by flannel, and kept in a warm place. The root hairs and root cap can be readily seen on these young roots.

AMŒBA.

Examination.—The readiest place to find some form or other of Amœba is in the slimy matter taken from decaying leaves in stagnant water. Mount in a drop of water and examine like Yeast.

COLOURLESS BLOOD-CORPUSCLES.

Examination.—Lay a drop of your own blood on a slide, then cover quickly with cover glass. By means of a camel-hair brush surround with oil to prevent evaporation.

VORTICELLA.

Examination.—On minute Water-plants, such as Duck-weed, groups are usually found. The operation of feeding may be observed by introducing particles of indigo or carmine into the water.

HYDRA.

Examination.—Found in stagnant pools and ditches. To examine alive, mount in plenty of water under a large coverglass.

Sections.—Kill by adding boiling water. Harden, prepare, and imbed as in Chara.

Sea-anemones treated in the same way might be used instead.

EARTH-WORM.

Dissection.—Kill with vapour of chloroform by placing in a stoppered bottle, with a few drops of chloroform. It then becomes stretched, and may be dissected under spirit. Fasten out in a dissecting dish, and with a fine pair of scissors slit it up longitudinally a little to one side of the saddle line and pin out the two flaps. Needles with brass heads for heads are best for pinning out.

FRESH-WATER MUSSEL.

Dissection.—Cut through adductor muscles of one side and remove the valve. Note the beating of the heart. Kill with hot water. Harden in spirit before following the course of the alimentary canal.

LOBSTER OR CRAYFISH.

Dissection.—Remove lateral portion of carapace by passing a knife under its free edge from the posterior end to cervical suture. This part of the carapace is the gill-cover or branchiostegite (Gr. *stego*, I cover). Notice scaphognathite working. Turn out the gills with the knife. Dissect from the left side, as in Pl. XIII. figs. 2 and 3.

Place another specimen under water in dissecting dish and it soon dies. Remove dorsal portion of carapace and of abdominal somites with scissors, in order to make out the chief organs, as in Pl. XIII. fig. 1.

Preparation of Skeleton.—Boil in strong potash solution, which dissolves everything but the chitin or horny substance composing the shell. The parts of the exo-skeleton may be disarticulated and laid out in their natural order.

SNAIL.

The Edible Snail is the largest of all the Snails, hence its convenience for study; but the Common Snail may be taken. Snails can be kept alive for a considerable time, and warm water generally makes them protrude from their shell. Boiling water kills them.

Dissection.—Remove shell bit by bit with strong forceps, and pin the animal out in spirit, dissecting from the dorsal surface. Lay open pulmonary chamber, then expose the viscera by laying open the dorsal integument of foot along middle line and removing the mantle. The viscera may next be laid out to display them to advantage.

FROG.

The Edible Frog is chosen on account of its larger size, but the Common Frog will also show the various points. Kill with chloroform.

Dissection.—A dissection from the ventral surface may be made under water in the dissecting dish by cutting through the skin in the middle line from the symphysis of lower jaw to symphysis of pubis; then pin out the skin on both sides, and various muscles, veins, etc., are brought into view. Next open abdomen a little to one side of anterior abdominal vein, cut through shoulder-girdle, and remove its central portion. The various viscera are then seen as in Pl. XVIII. fig. 2.

Turn over viscera to right side, cut away parts mentioned in Pl. XVIII. fig. 3 (text), and pin out with left side upwards so as to get the sectional view.

Prepare a specimen in spirit and nitric acid for the dissection of the nervous system. Dissect from dorsal surface, and remove the dorsal wall of the cerebro-spinal cavity by nipping it away with scissors, beginning at the junction of the skull and spinal column. Dissect out cranial nerves and the nerves of the limbs for a short distance. Remove brain and spinal cord and preserve in spirit for future use.

Take a similarly prepared specimen and dissect from ventral surface. Remove the bodies of the vertebræ and the floor of the skull. Along each side of the spinal column dissect out the sympathetic system, and trace its connection with the cranial and spinal nerves as in Pl. XX. diag. 1.

The principal cranial nerves may be dissected from the left side, as in Pl. XXI. fig. 5, after distending the gullet with a piece of glass tubing. Place in chromic acid, with a little nitric acid to hasten the softening of the bone and the hardening of the nerves.

Section of Spinal Cord.—Take a piece hardened in spirit, prepare and imbed in paraffin as before, and mount transverse sections in glycerine.

Circulation in Web.—In a thin piece of wood or cork make a notch to fit the web between two of the toes. Stretch the web over the notch by thread attached to the ends of the two toes. Keep the skin moist with wet blotting-paper, and after placing a small drop of water on the web, cover with triangular cover-glass for examination under high power.

Preparation of Skeleton.—After cleaning the bones roughly, steep for about a week in sufficient water to cover them, then place them for a few days in fresh water, which should be frequently renewed. They may be cleaned with a brush and then laid out in the sun to bleach. Any grease may be extracted from the bones by benzol.

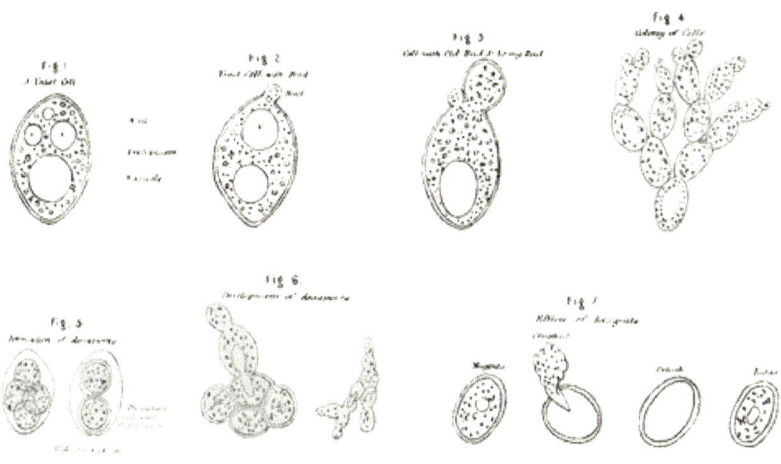

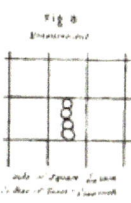

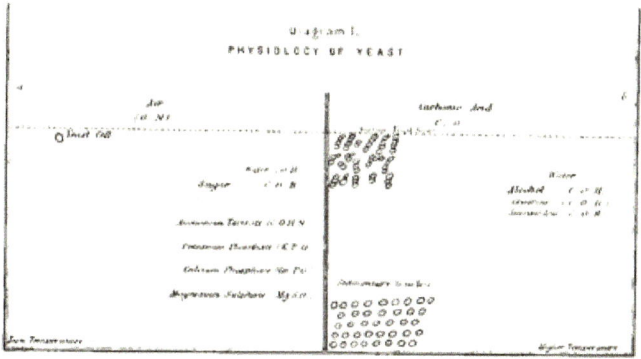

Diagram I.
PHYSIOLOGY OF YEAST

BACTERIA

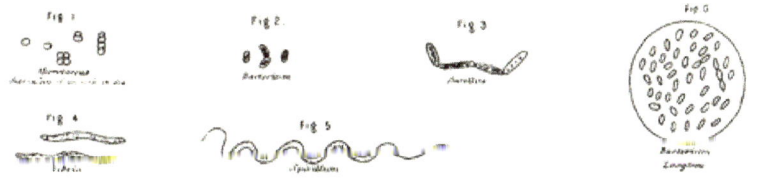

PLATE I.

THE YEAST PLANT.

Fig. 1. Showing—

A Cell
{ Cell-wall or sac.
{ Protoplasm (Gr. *protos*, first; *plasma*, from *plasso*, to mould).
{ Vacuole filled with cell-sap (L. *vacuum*, an empty space).

Figs. 2, 3, and 4. Showing—

MULTIPLICATION BY BUDDING OR GEMMATION (L. *gemma*, a bud).

The commencement of the process is seen in fig. 2. A bit of protoplasm is pushed out, stretching the cell-wall and making it thin. Fig. 4 shows a cell aggregate or colony produced by a repetition of the process of budding.

Fig. 5. Showing—

MULTIPLICATION BY ENDOGENOUS DIVISION (Gr. *endon*, within; *genao*, I produce).

The protoplasm collects usually into four round masses, each of which takes on a cell-wall. Cells produced in that way are called Ascospores (Gr. *askos*, a bag; *spora*, a seed) or Endoconidia (Gr. *endon*, within; *konis*, dust).

Fig. 6. Showing—

Ascospores set free by rupture of the cell-wall of parent, and multiplying by gemmation.

Fig. 7. Effect of—

Magenta—Stains protoplasm, leaving cell-wall comparatively unstained.

Crushing—Ruptures the cell-wall, and shows that the cell-wall is tough and resisting, while the protoplasm is semi-fluid.

Potash (KHO)—Dissolves out the protoplasm.

Iodine—Stains protoplasm.

Fig. 8. Measurement by eyepiece micrometer.

DIAGRAM I. PHYSIOLOGY—

a. Shows the composition of a fluid fit to nourish yeast (Pasteur's fluid).

Elements which make cell-wall (C.O.H.).

Elements which make protoplasm (C.O.H. N.).

Elements which make ash (P.S.K. Mg.Ca.)

b. Shows the composition of the fluid when acted upon by yeast. Process of fermentation (*ferveo*, I boil).

Sugar becomes
{ Carbonic acid (CO_2).
{ Alcohol.
{ Small quantities of succinic acid and glycerine.

About two per cent. of sugar is unaccounted for.

Ammonium tartrate, etc., used up by the yeast.

Total result
{ Manufacture of alcohol and carbonic acid.
{ Manufacture of cell-wall and protoplasm.

CLASSIFICATION OF YEAST.

Kingdom—Plants, because it possesses a cell-wall made of cellulose, and can manufacture protoplasm.

Sub-Kingdom—Thallophyta, because it possesses neither root, stem, nor leaf.

Class—Protophyta, because it has no sexual process of multiplication (Gr. *protos*, first; *phyton*, plant).

A

Group—Fungi, because it possesses no green colouring matter.
Order—Saccharomycetes (Gr. *sakcharon*, sugar ; *mukēs*, a fungus), because it requires a saccharine liquid for nourishment.
Genus—Saccharomy'ces.
Common Name—Yeast or Torula.

BACTERIA.

Fig. 1. Micrococci—Spherical (Gr. *mikros*, small ; *kokkos*, a berry), seen singly and together.
Fig. 2. Bacteria—Cylindrical (Gr. *bakterion*, a staff).
Fig. 3. Bacilli—Filiform and straight (L. *bacillum*, a little staff).
Fig. 4. Vibriones—Filiform and curved (L. *vibro*, I quiver).
Fig. 5. Spirillum—Spirally twisted.
    Note the threads of protoplasm at each end, cilia (L. *cilium*, an eyelash).
Fig. 6. The Zoogloea—Motionless Bacteria, embedded in gelatinous material (Gr. *zoon*, an animal, *plus*, glue).

CLASSIFICATION OF BACTERIA.

Kingdom—Plants.
Sub-Kingdom—Thallophyta.
Class—Protophyta.
Group—Fungi.
Order—Schizomycetes (Gr. *schizis*, a splitting), because they multiply by splitting.
Genera—Micrococcus, Bacterium, etc.

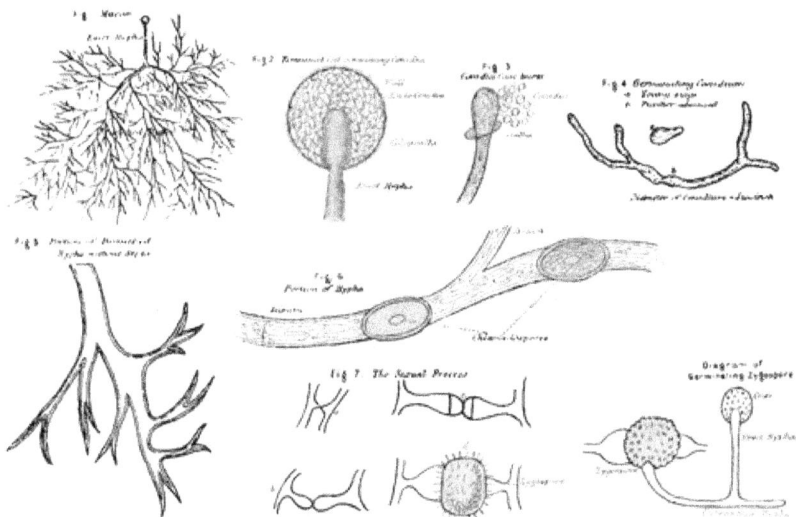

COMMON GREEN MOULD
(PENICILLIUM GLAUCUM)

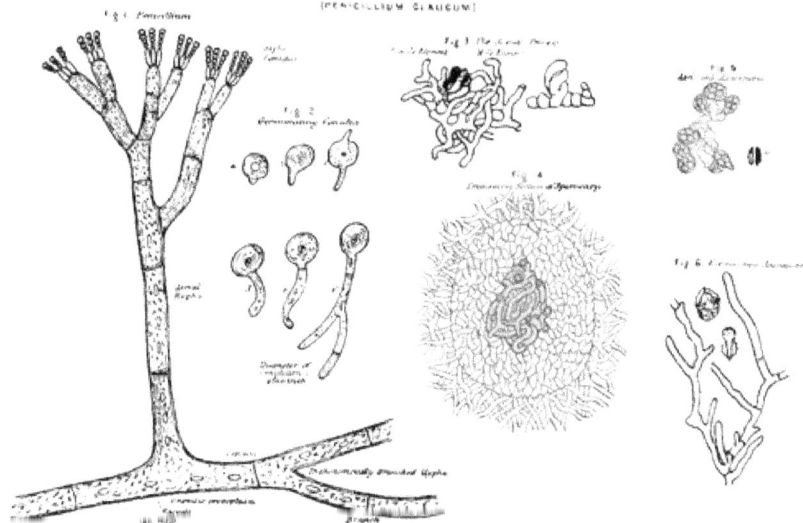

PLATE II.

COMMON BROWN MOULD.

Fig. 1. The Mucor Plant produced from a Conidium. Showing—
Branched hypha.
Erect hypha (Gr. *hyphé*, a weaving) terminating in a minute enlargement—the sporangium.

Fig. 2. Showing—
End of erect hypha.
Columella (L. a little column).
Terminal cell, conidia case, or sporangium (Gr. *spora*, a seed; *angeion*, a vessel).
Wall of sporangium with crystals of oxalate of lime.
Spores or endo-conidia (Gr. *endon*, within; *konis*, dust).

Fig. 3. Showing—
Burst conidia-case or sporangium.
Collar, the remains of the wall of sporangium.
Endo-conidia or spores.

Fig. 4. Showing—
The conidium germinating and producing a branched hypha, which ultimately develops into the form shown in fig. 1.

Fig. 5. Showing—
Portion of branched hypha with protoplasm removed.
No septa.

Fig. 6. Showing—
Portion of old submerged hypha, breaking up into distinct parts—the Chlamydospores (Gr. *chlamys*, a coat; *spora*, a seed) or Mucor-tonule, each containing a vacuole.
Note.—Vacuolated protoplasm and septum.

Fig. 7. The Sexual Process—
a & b. Two distinct processes given off from the hyphae.
c. Terminal cell separated off from each process.
d. Union of the two terminal cells to form a zygospore (Gr. *zygon*, a yoke; *spora*, a seed). Since the uniting elements closely resemble one another the process is called conjugation.

Diagram of the Pro-embryo of Mucor produced from a Zygospore. Showing—
Zygospore.
Unbranched hypha.
Erect hypha.
Conidia-case or sporangium, containing conidia, each of which can produce the Mucor plant (fig. 1).

CLASSIFICATION OF MUCOR.

Kingdom—Plantæ.
Sub-Kingdom—Thallophyta.
Class—Zygosporeæ, marked by its sexual process, viz. conjugation.
Group—Fungi.
Order—Zygomycetes.
Genus—Mucor.
Common Name—Brown Mould.

COMMON GREEN MOULD.

Fig. 1. Showing—

Dichotomously branched hypha (Gr. *dichotomia*, a division into two parts) subdivided by *septa*. Granular vacuolated protoplasm in the cells.

Aerial hypha, branching at its ends like a brush or pencil, hence the name Penicillium.

The terminal branches, corresponding to the hairs of the brush, breaking up into stylo-conidia (Gr. *stylos*, a stalk ; *konis*, dust).

Fig. 2. The Conidia. Showing—

Size—$\frac{1}{}$ inch in diameter.

Form—Spherical.

Structure—$\begin{cases} \text{Wall.} \\ \text{Protoplasm.} \\ \text{Vacuole.} \end{cases}$

Germination—

a & b. Eminence formed at one point of the conidium.

c. Eminences formed at two points.

d, e, & f. Elongation and subdivision of the eminences by septa.

Note.—The ultimate result of the growth of the conidium is to produce a Penicillium like that in fig. 1.

Fig. 3. Showing the Sexual Process.—

This has quite recently been made out, and occurs under peculiar conditions, as yet attained only by artificial means. The male element or antheridium (Gr. *anthos*, a flower ; *eidos*, form) is a short branch of a hypha, the female element or carpogonium (Gr. *carpos*, fruit ; *gone*, seed) also a short branch coiled like a corkscrew. These two elements come together and exercise on one another some reciprocal influence. A sexual process of this kind, where *the conjugating elements are different*, is called *Fertilisation*. As the result of fertilisation a fruit or sporocarp is produced, like a little pinhead. That fruit consists of an outer mass of sterile hyphæ enclosing a mass of fertile hyphæ. These fertile hyphæ are developed from the female element.

Fig. 4. Section of Sporocarp (Gr. *spora*, a seed ; *carpos*, fruit) or Fruit—

Sterile tissue.

Fertile tissue in centre (red).

Fig. 5. Portion of Fertile Tissue removed from Sporocarp. Showing—

a. Asci or cells containing spores (Gr. *askos*, a bag).

b. An ascospore removed from an ascus.

Fig. 6. Showing Germination of Ascospore.

CLASSIFICATION OF PENICILLIUM.

Kingdom—Plantæ.

Sub-Kingdom—Thallophyta.

Class—Carpospore, because it possesses a sporocarp.

Group—Fungi.

Order—Ascomycetes, because of the asci.

Genus—Penicillium (L. *penicillium*, a painter's brush).

Common Name—Green Mould.

PROTOCOCCUS PLUVIALIS

Diagram of Physiology

CHARA

PLATE III.

PROTOCOCCUS.

PROTOCOCCUS VULGARIS, the green scum on the bark of trees (Gr. *protos*, first ; *kokkos*, a berry).

Fig. 1. Showing—

A CELL { Cell-wall or sac.
Protoplasm containing green, sometimes red, chlorophyll (Gr. *chloros*, green ; *phyllon*, a leaf).

Fig. 2. Effect of—

    a. Iodine—Protoplasm stained and nucleus brought out.

    b. Iodine and sulphuric acid—The cell-wall becomes blue and the protoplasm coagulates The sulphuric acid converts cellulose into starch, and the iodine with starch forms the blue iodide of starch.

    c. Crushing causes rupture, and shows that the cell-wall is tough and resisting, while the protoplasmic contents are semi-fluid.

    d. Potash (KHO) dissolves out the protoplasmic contents.

Fig. 3. Showing MULTIPLICATION BY DIVISION —

    a. Division into two.

    b. Division into four.

    This process is the same as that which goes on at the growing point in the higher plants. (See Chara, fig. 4.)

Fig. 4. Showing MULTIPLICATION BY ENDOGENOUS DIVISION AND PRODUCTION OF MOTILE FORMS—

    a. The protoplasm has gathered itself up into a number of round masses, each of which is a zoospore or zoogonidium (Gr. *zoon*, alive ; *gone*, seed).

    b. A zoospore that has escaped from the parent cell. It consists of a naked mass of protoplasm, with two long vibratile protoplasmic threads or cilia by which it moves about.

PROTOCOCCUS PLUVIALIS, found in water-butts (L. *pluvia*, rain).

Fig. 1. RESTING FORM { Cell-wall.
Protoplasm.
Chlorophyll grains.

Fig. 2. PREPARATION FOR DIVISION.

Fig. 3. Showing RESULT OF DIVISION.

Fig. 4. MOTILE FORMS—ZOOSPORES OR ZOOGONIDIA —

    a. The protoplasm has drawn itself away from the cell-wall at all but two points At these points two vibratile cilia protrude through the cell-wall.

    b. A naked zoospore.

Fig. 5. EREMOSPHERA VIRIDIS, a close ally of Protococcus, containing starch granules —

    a. Unstained.

    b. Stained with iodine to bring out the starch granules.

    No starch is found in the Protococcus itself, probably because it uses up the starch as fast as it is manufactured.

DIAGRAM OF PHYSIOLOGY—

    a & *b.* Show that in the dark no oxygen is evolved from carbonic acid (CO_2).

    a & *c.* Show that in the light the carbonic acid is absorbed and oxygen gas given off.

    This process, viz. the absorption of CO_2 and evolution of O, is called *Assimilation.* Respiration is quite a different process ; it consists in the absorption of O and the evolution of CO_2. In the green plant these two processes go on together.

CLASSIFICATION OF PROTOCOCCUS.

Kingdom—Plants, because it possesses a cellulose wall, absorbs CO_2 and evolves O.
Sub-Kingdom—Thallophyta.
Group—Algæ.

CHARA.

Fig. 1 (*a*). Showing—

Axis . . .	{ Nodes (L. *nodus*, a knot). Internodes (L. *inter*, between).
Appendages	{ Leaves arranged in whorls. Branches.
Branch . .	{ Nodes. Internodes. Appendages.
Terminal Bud	{ Nodes with their leaves. Short internodes.

Fig. 1 (*b*). Showing the Cortical Layer investing the Internodal Cell (L. *cortex*, bark).

Fig. 2. Transverse Section of Internode. Showing—

Cortex.
Wall of internodal cell.
Protoplasm lining the wall, the so called primordial utricle (L. *primordium*, original; *utriculus*, a little bag).
Chlorophyll granules arranged so as to leave an uncoloured portion, the neutral line.
Inner layer of protoplasm—the moving layer.
Vacuole, filled with cell-sap.

Fig. 3. Showing the Node—

A surface of cells one layer thick.

Fig. 4. The Terminal Bud dissected to lay bare the Growing Point. Showing—

The hemispherical apical cell. It grows in length and multiplies by division transverse to the axis.
The cell immediately beneath apical cell afterwards divides transversely into two portions—the lower an internode, the upper a node.
The internodal cell (blue). It elongates, but does not divide at all.
The nodal cell (uncoloured). It does not elongate, but divides parallel to the axis, so as to form a transverse partition of cells.
Nodal cell originating a young leaf.
Nodal cell originating the cortex.

Fig. 5. Portion of Leaf. Showing—

The uncovered apical or terminal cell.
Nodal cell.
Cortex { Descending lobes. Ascending lobes.

Fig. 6. Movements of the Protoplasm—

The arrows represent the direction of the currents of protoplasm.
The uncoloured bands are the neutral lines (see fig. 2).

Diagram I. Showing Formation of Cortex.

The peripheral cells of the node (shown in fig. 3) send pockets upwards and downwards to form the ascending and descending cortical lobes.

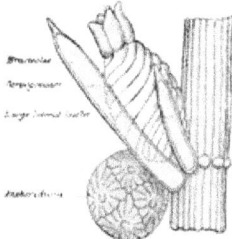

Fig 1. Portion of Leaf with node & female organs

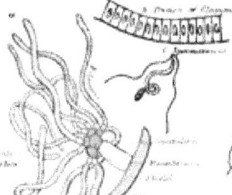

Fig 2. Structure of Antheridium

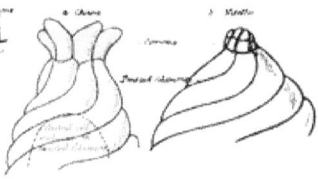

Fig 3. Structure of Carpogonium

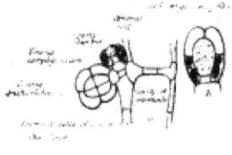

Fig 4. Development of Carpogonium

Fig 5. Germinating Carpogonium

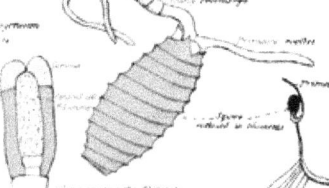

Diagram 1.

THE BRACKEN FERN. PTERIS AQUILINA.

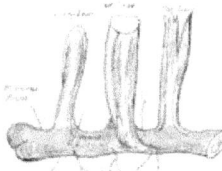

Fig 1. Plate of a fern

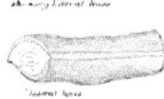

Fig 2. Portion of Rhizome shewing Lateral buds

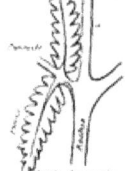

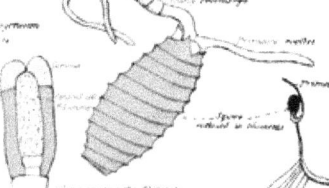

Fig 3. Parts of leaf

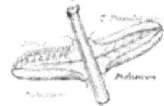

Fig 4. Pinnule

Fig 5. Sporangia

Fig 6. Spore

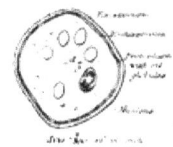

Fig 7. Development of spore

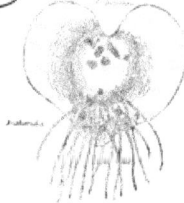

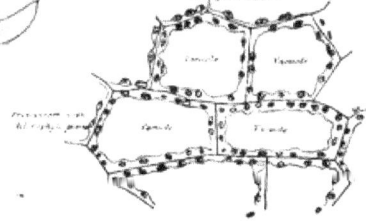

Fig 8. Portion of Prothallus

PLATE IV.

CHARA—*continued.*

Fig. 1. PORTION OF LEAF. Showing—
    Antheridium, male organ, or globule.
    Carpogonium, female organ, nucule, sporangium, or spore-fruit (Gr. *spora*, a seed ; *angeion*, a
    vessel).
Fig. 2. THE ANTHERIDIUM DISSECTED. Showing—
    a. Shield.
    Manubrium (L. a handle).
    Capitulum (L. a little head) (blue).
    Secondary capitula (blue). Not named on drawing.
    Filaments.
    b. Portion of filament, with a spermatozoid in each of its cells.
    c. A liberated spermatozoid, with two long cilia.
Fig. 3. THE CARPOGONIUM OR NUCULE.—
    Central cell.
    Twisted filaments, quite different from the filaments of the antheridium.
    The one-celled corona in Chara, and the two-celled corona in Nitella.
Fig. 4. DEVELOPMENT OF THE CARPOGONIUM OR SPORE-FRUIT. Sectional view.
Fig. 5 and DIAGRAM I. Showing DEVELOPMENT OF THE STOCK, enclosed in sporocarp—
    Proembryo.
    Pseudo-whorl of leaves, with the Chara in its axil.

CLASSIFICATION OF CHARACEÆ.

Kingdom—Plantæ.
Sub-Kingdom—Thallophyta (exceptional in having axis and appendages).
Class—Carpospore, because it has a spore fruit.
Group—Algæ.
Order—Characeæ.
Genera—Chara and Nitella.

THE BRACKEN FERN.

Fig. 1. Showing—
    LEAVES { Rudimentary leaf. / Young leaf. / Cut leaf. / Old leaf.
    Underground stem or rhizome (Gr. *rhiza*, a root ; *onos*, the same as) with its growing point.
    Roots.

Fig. 2. LATERAL LINES OF RHIZOME.

Fig. 3. Showing—

    a. PART OF LEAF OR FROND   { Rachis (Gr. *rachis*, a spine, ridge).
                                            { Pinna (L. a feather).
                                            { Pinnule (L. *pinnula*, a little feather).

    b. TWO PINNULES VIEWED FROM BELOW { Indusium (L. *induere*, to clothe) covering spore-cases.
                                            { Sorus (Gr. *soros*, a heap), a cluster of spore-cases.

Fig. 4. Showing FORKED VENATION AND INDUSIUM.

Fig. 5. SPORE-CASE OR SPORANGIUM. Showing—

    Stalk.
    Case.
    Annulus (L. a ring).   In *c*, a small part below the spores is inadvertently uncoloured.
    Spores.

Fig. 6. SPORE. Showing—

    Exosporium (Gr. *exo*, outside ; *spora*, a seed).
    Endosporium (Gr. *endon*, within ; *spora*, a seed).
    Protoplasm with oil-globules.
    Nucleus.

Fig. 7. DEVELOPMENT OF SPORE. Showing—

    a. Endosporium protruded.
    b. Divided to form a young prothallus, with root-hairs.
    c. Old prothallus with root-hairs, male organs or antheridia, and female organs or archegonia
        (Gr. *archos*, chief ; *gone*, seed).

Fig. 8. PROTHALLUS UNDER HIGH POWER. Showing—

    CELLS .   .   .   . { Cell-wall.
                                            { Protoplasm.
                                            { Chlorophyll granules.
                                            { Large vacuoles filled with cell-sap.

PLATE V.

FERN—continued.

Fig. 1. The Antheridium and Antherozoids of the Royal Fern (Osmunda Regalis), under surface of prothallus (green).

Fig. 2. The Archegonium with its Central Cell or Germ-cell.

Fig. 3. Division of Central Cell into Four in the Bracken.

Fig. 4. Connection of young Bracken Fern with its Prothallus by means of the Foot.

Figs. 5, 6. Transverse and Longitudinal Sections of the Rhizome. Showing:
  S., Outer sclerenchyma (Gr. skleros, hard; enchuma, tissue).
  G. T. Ground tissue or parenchyma (Gr. para, together; enchuma, tissue).
  F. V. B. Fibro-vascular bundles—outer.
  S., Inner sclerenchyma.
  G. T. Ground tissue.
  F. V. B. Fibro-vascular bundles—inner.

Fig. 7. Transverse and Longitudinal Sections of Rhizome. Showing—
  Epidermis, sub-epidermis, and parenchyma loaded with starch granules.
  Fibro-vascular bundle with scalariform and spiral vessels.
  Parenchyma with starch.
  Sclerenchyma very thick walled (Gr. skleros, hard).

Fig. 8. Portion of Fibro-vascular Bundle. Showing—
  Cells of fibro-vascular bundle-sheath.
  Cells of bast sheath with starch granules.

  Bast or Phloem { Bast fibres or hard bast.
                  { Bast vessels.   } Soft bast.
                  { Bast parenchyma or procambium.   }

  Wood or Xylem { Scalariform vessels.
                { Spiral vessels.
                { Wood parenchyma.

  Note.—In the complete bundle the bast forms a ring surrounding the wood.

Fig. 9. Part of an Oblique Section of a Leaf-stalk. Showing the scalariform vessels (L. scala, a ladder) of the bundle.

CLASSIFICATION OF FERN.

Kingdom—Plants.

Sub-Kingdom—Vascular Cryptogams (Gr. kruptos, hidden; gamos, a marriage). Vascular, because they possess fibro-vascular bundles; cryptogams, because the sexual organs are hidden on an inconspicuous prothallus.

Class—Filicium.

Order—Filices.

Genus—Pteris (Gr. pteron, a wing).

Species—Aquilina (L. aquila, an eagle).

Common Name—Bracken Fern.

B

PLATE VI.

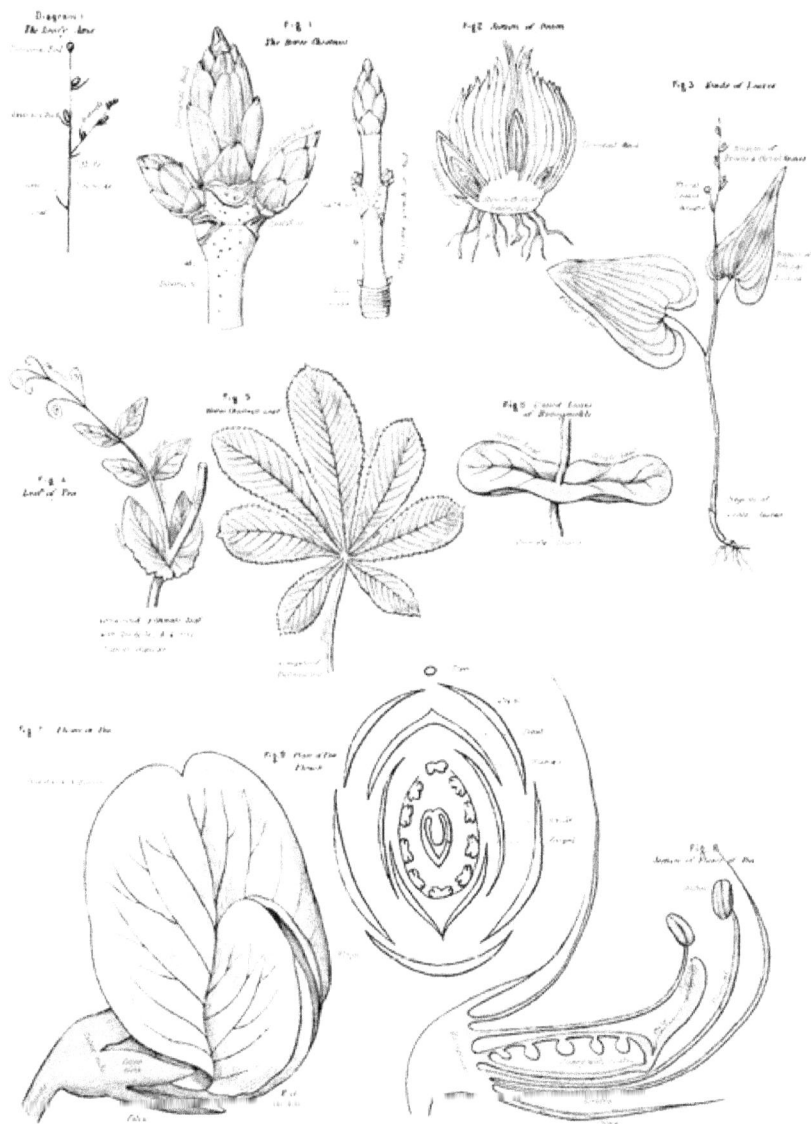

THE FLOWERING PLANT.

DIAGRAM I. Showing—

STEM . . . . . . { Nodes, bearing leaves (L. *nodus*, a knot).
{ Internodes, bearing no leaves (L. *inter*, between ; *nodus*, a knot).

APPENDAGES OF STEM { Leaf.
{ Bud, a shortened stem with crowded leaves.
{ Branch, an expanded bud.

POSITION OF BUDS . { Axillary, in the angle between the leaf and stem (L. *axilla*, the armpit).
{ Terminal.

FIG. 1 (*a*). THE HORSE CHESTNUT. Showing—

Internodes.
Nodes with leaf-scars.
Two axillary buds.
Terminal bud.

FIG. 1 (*b*). THE SAME. Showing the scars left by the falling off of the bud-scales. These scars mark the commencement of a year's growth.

FIG. 2. BULB OF ONION. Showing—

Stem, short.
Leaves, crowded, and stored with nutriment.
Buds (1) terminal and (2) axillary.
Roots, fibrous.

The peculiarity of the Onion is this : it remains permanently in the bud condition. A permanent bud of that kind is called a bulb.

FIG. 3. Showing KINDS OF LEAVES—

Scale leaves.
Foliage leaves— the green leaves which manufacture starch (L. *folium*, the leaf).
Bracts—leaves near flowers (L. *bractea*, a thin plate).
Floral leaves (L. *flos*, a flower). (Red.)

FIGS. 4, 5. EXAMPLES OF LEAVES—

Pinnate leaf, with elongated midrib (Pea).
Palmate leaf, with extremely short midrib (Horse Chestnut).
Compound leaf. The incisions extending into the midrib, and subdividing one leaf into a number of leaflets.
Stipules—appendages originating from the base of leaf-stalk, not from the stem.

FIG. 6. Showing FOLIAGE LEAVES united or connate (L. *con*, together ; *natus*, born).

FIG. 7. FLOWER OF PEA. Showing—

Sepal leaves united below (gamosepalous calyx).
Petal leaves of unequal size (irregular corolla indicated in formula by -).

FIG. 8. Showing GENERAL STRUCTURE OF THE FLOWER—

Calyx (Gr. *kalyx*, a cup).
Corolla (L. *corolla*, a little crown).
Stamens or Andrœcium { Filament (L. *filum*, a thread).
(Gr. *aner*, male; *oikos*, { Anther containing pollen-grains.
house) (male organs) {
Pistil or Gynœcium (Gr. { Ovary containing ovules.
gune, female ; *oikos*, { Style.
house (female organs) { Stigma (Gr. *stigma*, a brand).

FIG. 9. PLAN OF PEA FLOWER. Showing—

Calyx = five sepal leaves united.
Corolla = five petal leaves separate.
Andrœcium = ten stamen leaves, nine united and one free.
Gynœcium = one carpel leaf.

Formula ⚥ Ca. (5), Co. 5, An. (9) + 1 Gn. 1.

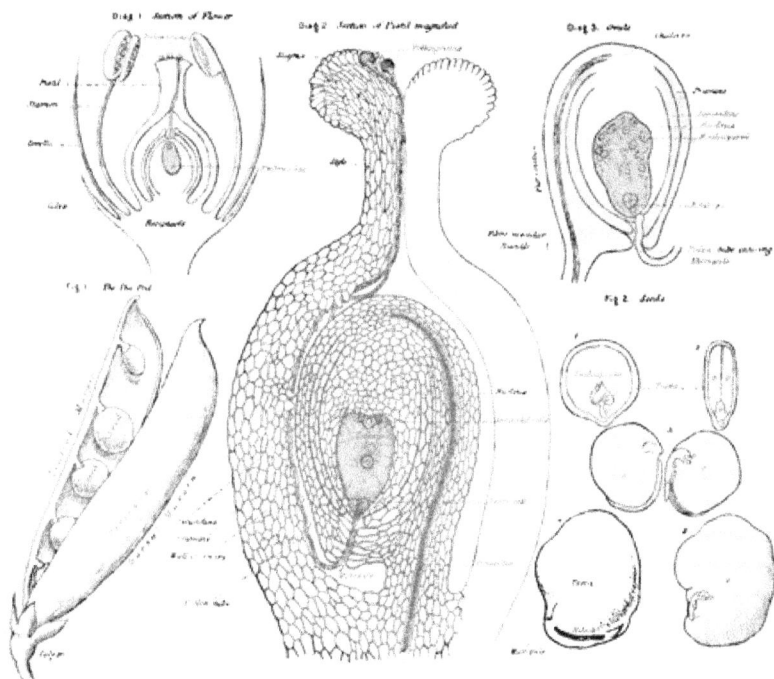

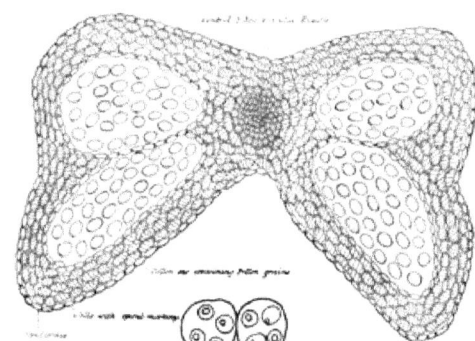

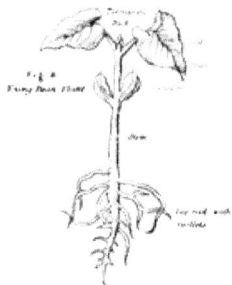

PLATE. VII.

THE FLOWERING PLANT.

DIAGRAM I. Showing—

RECEPTACLE OR THALAMUS TO WHICH THE FLORAL LEAVES ARE ATTACHED.

INSERTIONS OF FLORAL LEAVES . . . . .
- Calyx, hypogynous or inferior (Gr. *hupo*, under; *gune*, the female organ).
- Corolla, hypogynous or inferior.
- Stamens, hypogynous.
- Ovary, superior or free, containing an erect ovule.

DIAGRAM II. Showing—

PISTIL OR GYNŒCIUM . .
- Stigma, for receiving pollen.
- Style.
- Ovary, containing one ovule

IMPREGNATION OF OVULE — Pollen-grains attached to stigma and throwing out pollen-tubes, which make their way down the style, enter the micropyle of the ovule, and fertilize the germ-cell in the embryo-sac.

DIAGRAM III. Showing—

OVULE . . . .
- Primine or outer coat (L. *primus*, first), formed after inner coat.
- Secundine or inner coat (L. *secundus*, second).
- Nucleus, with a giant cell—the embryo-sac.

EMBRYO-SAC FERTILIZED
- Wall of sac.
- Embryo.
- Endosperm.

FIG. 1. Showing the RIPE PISTIL OF PEA—
PERICARP—Ripe wall of ovary, dry and splitting into two valves.
SEED—Ripe ovule.

FIG. 2. Showing SEEDS—

1. NUX VOMICA (Albuminous Seed)
- Testa or seed-skins (L. *testa*, a shell).
- Endosperm, the so-called albumen (Gr. *endon*, within; *sperma*, a seed)
- Embryo, with two cotyledons, or seed-leaves.

2. ALMOND (Exalbuminous Seed)
- Testa.
- Endosperm absorbed into embryo.
- Embryo, with two cotyledons.

3. PEA (Exalbuminous Seed).

4 and 5. BEAN (Exalbuminous Seed)
- Testa.
- Endosperm absorbed.
- Embryo, with two cotyledons.

EMBRYO . . . . . .
- Cotyledons.
- Plumule.
- Radicle.

FIG. 3. ANTHER OF TULIP, showing fibro-vascular bundle in centre corresponding to the midrib of the leaf. Right anther-lobe with two pollen-sacs. Left anther-lobe with two pollen-sacs.

DIAGRAM IV. FORMATION OF POLLEN-GRAINS BY ENDOGENOUS DIVISION.

FIG. 4. YOUNG BEAN PLANT, showing—

AXIS . . . .
- Tap-root.
- Stem with terminal bud.

APPENDAGES
- Rootlets.
- 2 Cotyledons.
- Foliage leaves.

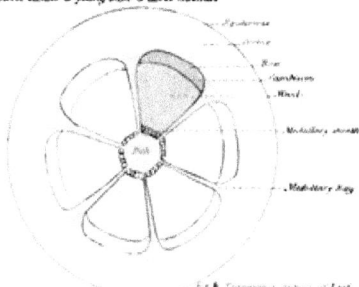

Fig 1. Transverse section of young stem of Horse chestnut

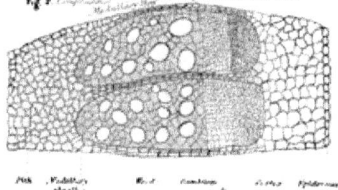

Fig 1. Transverse section of young Horse chestnut stem

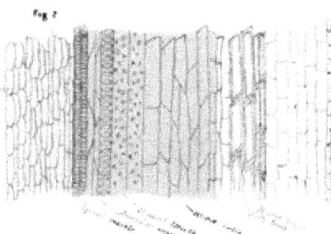

Fig 2

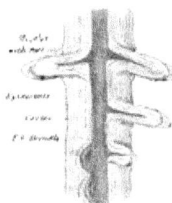

Fig 3. Longitudinal section of Root of Bean

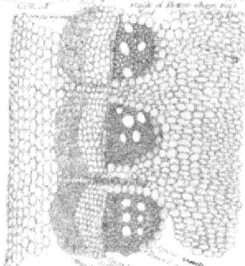

Fig 6. Transverse section of Leaf

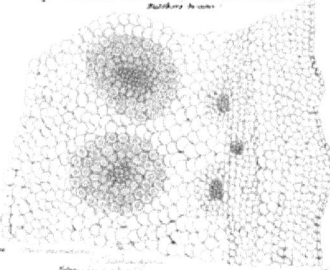

Fig 3. Transverse section of stem of Bean

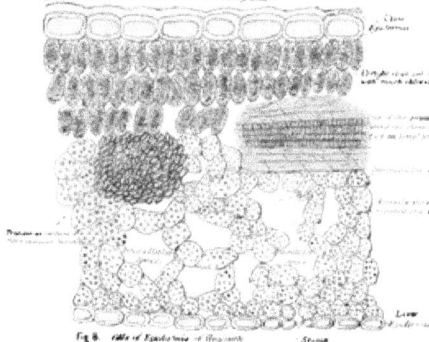

Fig 7. Transverse section of Leaf blade of Cherry Laurel

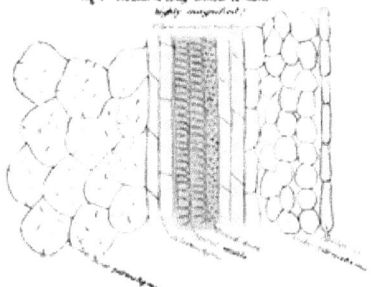

Fig 4. Portion of Long section of stem highly magnified

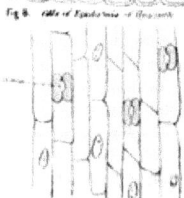

Fig 8. Cells of Epidermis of Hyacinth   Stoma

PLATE VIII.

HISTOLOGY OF FLOWERING PLANT.

Stem—

 Diag. 1. Transverse Section of a one-year-old stem of Horse Chestnut—
  Pith or medulla in centre.
  Fibro-vascular bundles arranged in a ring round the pith—
   Wood or xylem, including medullary sheath.
   Cambium, a soft cellular layer.
   Bast or phloem outside the cambium.
  Cortex, connected with the pith by the medullary rays.
  Epidermis.

  Note.—The part of the stem outside the soft cambium is readily removable, and is the separable bark.

 Fig. 1. Transverse Section of same stem under the microscope—
  Pith, consisting of parenchyma cells.
  Fibro-vascular bundle—
   Wood or xylem—
    Vessels, large openings.
    Wood-cells between the vessels.
   Cambium, small thin-walled cells.
   Bast or phloem—
    Soft portion, made up of thin walled cells.
    Hard portion, or liber layer, made up of round thick-walled cells, the central cavity
     being almost obliterated.
  Medullary rays, brick-shaped cells between the fibro-vascular bundles.
  Cortex, angular cells, parenchyma.
  Epidermis, a single layer of squarish cells.
 Fig. 2. Long. Section of the Horse Chestnut stem—
  Pith-cells.
  Fibro-vascular bundle—
   Wood—
    Spiral vessels of medullary sheath, elongated tubes with spirally thickened walls.
    Annular vessels, elongated tubes with ringlike thickenings.
    Dotted ducts, elongated tubes thickened so as to leave thin places, the dots.
    Wood-cells, elongated, and when older with thick walls, and then called woody
     fibres or wood prosenchyma.
   Cambium, thin-walled cells.
   Bast—
    Soft bast, elongated thin-walled cells.
    Hard bast, thick-walled and elongated cells forming the flexible bast fibres.
  Cortex, parenchymatous cells.
  Epidermis, a single layer of cells.
 Figs. 3, 4. Sections of stem of Butcher's Broom magnified—
  Differences from Horse Chestnut stem—
   Fibro-vascular bundles are not arranged in a ring round pith, but scattered irregu-
    larly.
   No cambium and therefore no provision for increase after first year.

Root—

Fig. 5. Long. Section of root of Bean plant—

Root . . . . . . { Central fibro-vascular bundle, surrounded by cortical parenchyma and epidermis.

Epidermis, one layer thick ; at tip of root split into several layers forming the root-cap or pileorhiza (L. *pileus*, a cap ; Gr. *rhiza*, a root).

Rootlets . . . . { Appendages of the root developed endogenously (Gr. *endon*, within ; *gennao*, I produce), and repeating the structure of the main root.

Leaf—

Fig. 6. The Stalk or Petiole of Horse Chestnut leaf—
Repeats the characters of the one-year-old stem.

Fig. 7. The Leaf Blade or Lamina of the Cherry Laurel—

Epidermis . . . . { Upper epidermis, colourless, a single layer, with the outer walls thickened forming cuticle.

Lower epidermis, like upper epidermis, but stomata more abundant.

Ground or Cortical Parenchyma . . . { Palisade tissue.

Loose tissue with less chlorophyll.

Fibro-vascular bundles, forming veins.

Fig. 8. Epidermis of Hyacinth—
Stoma, the opening (Gr. *stoma*, a mouth).
Guard-cells (red), two surrounding each stoma.

CLASSIFICATION OF PEA OR BEAN PLANT.

Sub-Kingdom—Phanerogamia, because the sexual organs are conspicuous (Gr. *phaneros*, visible ; *gamos*, sexual union).

Class—Dicotyledon—
The young plant has two cotyledons (Pl. VII. fig. 4).
The fibro-vascular bundles form a ring round the pith (Pl. VIII. diag.).
Leaf has reticulated venation.
Flower leaves arranged in fives (Pl. VI. fig. 9).

Order—Leguminosæ, distinguished by the arrangement of the corolla leaves, and the fruit a pod or legume.

Genera—Pisum (pea), Vicia (bean).

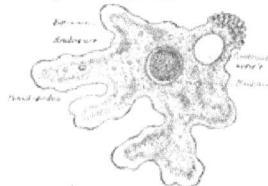

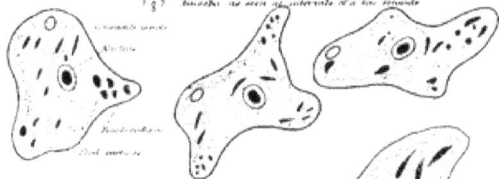

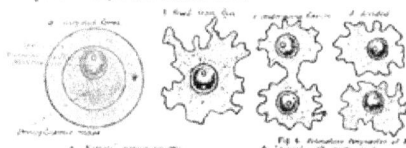

BELL ANIMALCULE (VORTICELLA)

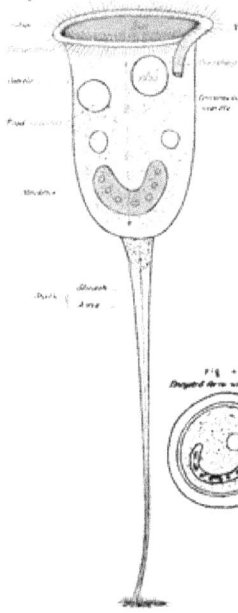

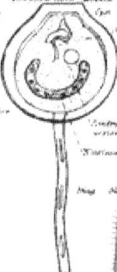

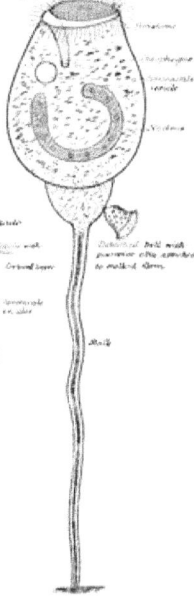

PLATE IX.

PROTEUS ANIMALCULE.

STRUCTURE.—

 FIG. 1. Ectosarc or outer transparent border (Gr. *ektos*, outside ; *sarx*, flesh).

  Endosarc or inner granular portion (Gr. *endon*, within).

  Contractile vesicle or vacuole, a cavity filled with a clear fluid.

  Nucleus or endoplast, a roundish solid granular portion of protoplasm.

  Pseudopodia (Gr. *pseudos*, false ; *pous*, *podos*, a foot), processes of the body constantly changing

MOVEMENTS.—

 FIG. 2. Changes of form constantly taking place, hence the name of Proteus Animalcule.

  Food-particles.

MULTIPLICATION.—

 FIG. 3, *a*. Stationary form surrounded by a structureless case or cyst.

  b. Mobile form escaped from cyst.

  c. Process of fission taking place.

  d. Original amoeba divided into two.

CLASSIFICATION.— Structural relations with other animals.

  Kingdom—Animalia, because it depends on pre-formed protoplasm and does not possess a cellulose cell-wall.

  Sub-Kingdom—Protozoa (Gr. *protos*, first ; *zoon*, an animal), because it is not differentiated into cells.

  Natural Order—Protoplasta (Gr. *plastos*, moulded), because it possesses a nucleus and contractile vesicle.

  Genus—Amoeba (Gr. *amoibe*, change).

  Common Name—Proteus Animalcule.

COLOURLESS CORPUSCLES OF HUMAN BLOOD.

 FIG. 4, *a*. Structure—granular with spherical or irregular outline.

  b. Nucleus brought out with dilute acetic acid.

  c. Amoeboid movements taking place sluggishly.

BELL ANIMALCULE.

STRUCTURE—

Fig. 1. Bell-shaped body with slender stalk for attachment.

Body
{
Cuticle, a very thin layer of protoplasm investing the body.

Disc, covering the mouth of bell and fringed with cilia.

Peristome (Gr. *peri*, around; *stoma*, a mouth), the ciliated rim separated from the edge of the disc by a groove.

Vestibulum (L. an entrance), a depression in the groove where food enters by a permanent mouth. The undigested matter passes out by a temporary anus (L. a vent).

Œsophagus or gullet, leading from vestibule into the soft body-substance.

Food-vacuoles, food-particles enveloped in water and dropped off from the end of the gullet.

Contractile vesicle.

Curved nucleus.
}

Stalk
{
Sheath, a continuation of the cuticle.

Axis, the central muscular fibre.
}

DIAGRAM OF THE PARAMŒCIUM OR SLIPPER ANIMALCULE, A FREE-SWIMMING INFUSORIAN—

Cuticle and cilia.

Cortical layer with two contractile vesicles.

Body-substance like soft-boiled sago.

Funnel-shaped mouth opening by a short gullet into body-substance.

Anus, merely a temporary opening.

MOVEMENTS—

Fig. 2. The spirally-coiled stalk, the retracted disc, and the curved-in peristome.

Figs. 3, 4. Encysted forms—stalked and unstalked.

MULTIPLICATION—

Fig. 5. Longitudinal fission; a bell divides lengthways into two, and the detached portion finally becomes like the original.

REPRODUCTION—

Fig. 6. A free-swimming bell fuses with a stalked form, producing a single individual; this is the so-called process of conjugation. The attached bell was formerly taken for a bud. (Posterior cilia not shown.)

CLASSIFICATION—

Sub-Kingdom—Protozoa.

Natural Order—Infusoria, because it possesses an outer layer (ectosarc) provided with cilia and contractile vesicle or vesicles, and an inner substance (endosarc) with nucleus, and usually with a mouth leading into it and an anus leading out. They occur in infusions, hence the name.

Genus—Vorticella, so named from the vortex caused by the moving cilia.

Common Name—Bell Animalcule.

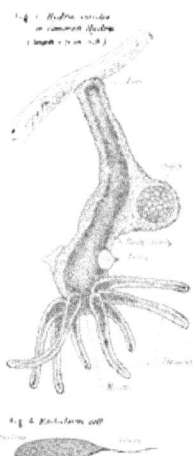

Diagram — Longitudinal Section of Hydra

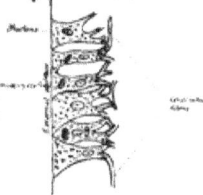

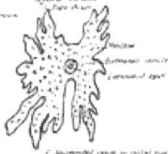

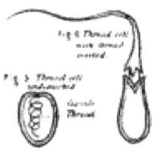

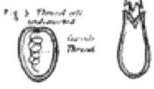

Diagram 2 — Development of Hydrozoa

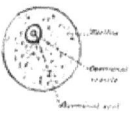

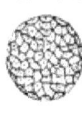

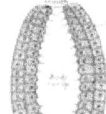

EARTH WORM (LUMBRICUS TERRESTRIS)

Fig 1. — Earthworm

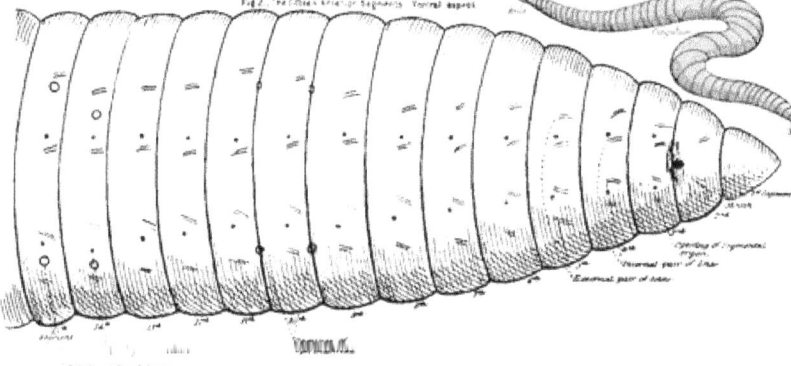

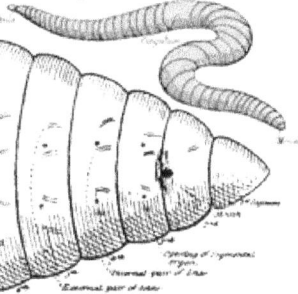

PLATE X.

FRESH-WATER POLYPE.

GENERAL CHARACTERS—

Figs. 1, 2. Foot or hydrorhiza (Gr. *rhiza*, root) attached to some floating body.
Mouth at free end.
Tentacles or feelers (L. *tentare*, to feel) surrounding the mouth.
Reproductive organs { Testis, the male organ.
{ Ovary, the female organ.
Multiplication by budding or gemmation (fig. 2).

GENERAL STRUCTURE—

Diag. 1. Ectoderm (Gr. *ektos*, outside; *derma*, skin) (red).
Endoderm (Gr. *endon*, within).
Body-cavity, serving also as a digestive cavity, and continued into the tentacles.

MINUTE STRUCTURE OR HISTOLOGY—

Fig. 3. Ectoderm-cells with contractile prolongations—neuro-muscular cell layer.
Nuclei and nematocysts in the cells.
Fig. 4. Endoderm-cell with cilium on its inner surface.
Figs. 5, 6. Thread-cells or nematocysts (Gr. *nema*, thread; *kustos*, a bag), consisting of capsule, filament, and three recurved spines at base of thread.

REPRODUCTION OR SEXUAL PROCESS—

Fig. 7, *a*. Spermatozoon (Gr. *sperma*, seed; *zoon*, an animal) with oval head and vibratile cilium.
b. Ripe ovum, consisting of vitellus or yolk, germinal vesicle or nucleus, and germinal spot or nucleolus.
c. Impregnated ovum divided into a number of cells, surrounded by a capsule—burst to show the contents.

MULTIPLICATION OR ASEXUAL PROCESS—

Process of gemmation shown in fig. 2.

DEVELOPMENT OF HYDROZOA—

Diag. 2. The impregnated *ovum* by division becomes a mulberry-like mass or *morula*, the morula becomes hollow by the accumulation of fluid in its interior, forming a *planula*, and the planula by gradual thinning opens at one end, becoming the so-called *gastrula*, which passes into the mature form.

Note.—In the Hydra itself there is no proper planula stage, as the two-layered form represented in the morula.

CLASSIFICATION—

Sub-Kingdom—Coelenterata (Gr. *koilos*, hollow; *enteron*, an intestine), because it is composed of two cell-layers—ectoderm and endoderm—and has no cavity separate from the body-cavity.
Natural Order—Hydrozoa, because a digestive sac is not marked off from the body-cavity, and the reproductive organs are external.
Genus—Hydra.
Common Name—Fresh-water Polype (Gr. *polus*, many; *pous*, a foot).

THE EARTH-WORM.

EXTERNAL CHARACTERS—

Fig. 1. The segmented body with a mouth at one end, an anus at the other, and a swollen portion called the cingulum (L. a girdle) or clitellum (L. *clitella*, a saddle).
Fig. 2. Mouth situated on the 2nd segment.
External and internal pair of setae (L. *seta*, bristle).
Openings of segmental organs, one on each side of all the segments except the two first.
Openings of spermatheca or receptacles of the spermatozoa (Gr. *sperma*, seed; *theke*, a repository).
Openings of vasa deferentia (L. excretory ducts) on ventral face of little segment.
Openings of oviduct on ventral face of 14th segment.

PLATE XI.

THE EARTH-WORM—*continued.*

DISPOSITION OF INTERNAL ORGANS—

FIG. 1 and DIAGRAM—

ALIMENTARY SYSTEM . . .	Mouth.
	Cut end of muscular pharynx.
	Gullet.
	Crop, a dilated portion of gullet.
	Gizzard, whitish, thick, and muscular.
	Intestine leading straight to anus, and covered with a brownish mass supposed to be the liver.
BLOOD SYSTEM—CIRCULATORY AND RESPIRATORY . .	Colourless corpuscles in perivisceral cavity—two shown.
	Pseud-hæmal vessels contractile, and therefore circulatory—
	Supra-intestinal vessel (L. *supra*, above).
	Sub-intestinal vessel (L. *sub*, under).
	Sub-neural vessel.
	Commissural vessels connecting supra-intestinal and sub-intestinal vessels.
	Dilated commissural vessels in the region of the reproductive organs, the so-called hearts.
	Coloured fluid without corpuscles contained in pseud-hæmal vessels acts as an oxygen-carrier, and is therefore respiratory in function.
RENAL SYSTEM	Segmental organs in pairs in each segment.
NERVOUS SYSTEM	Cerebral or præ-oral ganglia connected by commissural cords embracing the pharynx with the
	Sub-œsophageal or post-oral ganglia which form the anterior extremity of a
	Chain of ganglia extending to end of body.
REPRODUCTIVE SYSTEM . .	Ovaries and oviducts.
	Testes and vasa deferentia shown in *fig.* 2.

FIGS. 2, 3, 4. RENAL AND REPRODUCTIVE SYSTEMS—

Segmental organs with internal ciliated opening and external pore (fig. 3).

Anterior pair of spermathecæ.
Posterior pair of spermathecæ.
Anterior pair of bilobed testes.
Posterior pair of testes.
Anterior reservoir of testes with duct.
Posterior reservoir of testes with duct.
Common vasa deferentia.
Capsulo-genous glands for secreting egg-capsules.
Ovaries.
Oviducts with wide ciliated internal opening and external opening (fig. 4).

FIG. 5. Ovary with ova. When laid the eggs are enclosed in clusters within a chitinous case, each egg consisting of—Vitelline membrane.
Vitellus.
Germinal vesicle.
Germinal spot.

Spermatozoa from Spermathecæ.

CLASSIFICATION—

Sub-Kingdom—Annelida (L. *annulus*, a ring), because the body is segmented; without jointed limbs; nervous system forms a ring round gullet, followed by a ventral chain of ganglia.
Natural Order—Oligochæta (Gr. *oligos*, few; *chaite*, hair), because the bristles are in rows, not tufted.
Genus—Lumbricus.
Common Name—Earth-worm.

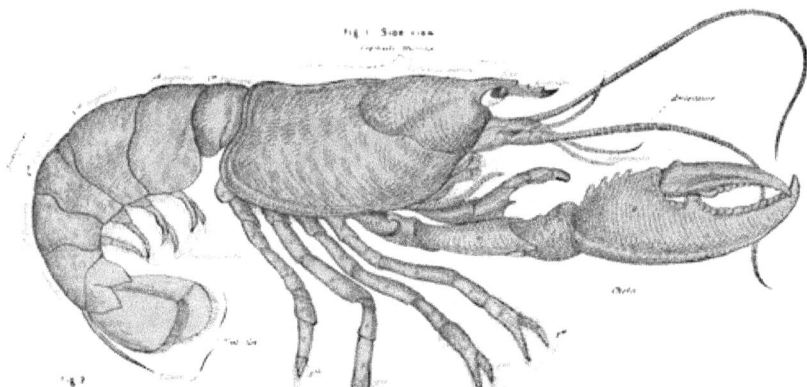

Fig 1 Side view

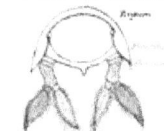

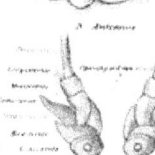

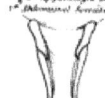

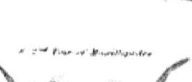

PLATE XII

LOBSTER AND CRAYFISH.

EXTERNAL CHARACTERS—

FIG. 1. ENTIRE SPECIMEN—

Ce'phalo-thorax (Gr. *kephale*, head ; *thorax*, a breast-plate) covered by Carapace . . . {
Cervi'cal suture between head and thorax.
Frontal spine or rostrum (L. the beak), a prolongation in front.

Abdo'men—six segments and a backward prolongation, the telson (Gr. a limit).

APPENDAGES {
Cephalic.
Thoracic, including great claws or chelæ and ambulatory limbs.
Abdominal, including the swimmerets.

FIG. 2. THIRD ABDOMINAL SOMITE—

BODY-SEGMENT {
Tergum (L. the back) or dorsal portion.
Pleuron (Gr. a side).
Sternum (Gr. *sternon*, the breast) or ventral portion.

APPENDAGES {
Proto'podite or basal portion (red).
Exo'podite or outer terminal portion (blue).
Endo'podite or inner terminal portion (yellow).

FIG. 3. SIXTH ABDOMINAL SOMITE AND TELSON ; *a*, Lobster ; *b*, Crayfish—
Exopodite divided transversely into two pieces.
Telson divided transversely in Crayfish, undivided in Lobster.

FIGS. 4, 5. APPENDAGES OF FIRST AND SECOND ABDOMINAL SOMITES IN THE MALE—
FIG. 4. Endopodite, bearing a small inner process.
FIG. 5. Exopodite gone.
Endopodites grooved inwardly, so that the two scooped portions brought together form a kind of channel.

FIG. 6. APPENDAGES IN ORDER—

HEAD—six pair {
1. Ophthalmites or eye-stalks (Gr. *ophthalmos*, the eye).
2. Anten'nules with opening of auditory sac.
3. Anten'næ or feelers with opening of green gland.
4. Mandibles (L. *mando*, I chew).
5. Maxillæ, first pair.
6. Maxillæ, second pair with boat-shaped scaphognathite (Gr. *skaphe*, a boat ; *gnathos*, a jaw) for baling out and drawing in water (blue and green).

THORAX—right pair {
Maxillipedes or foot-jaws—
7. First pair, epipodite (green) without a gill.
8. Second pair, epipodite gill-bearing.
9. Third pair, epipodite gill-bearing.
Chelæ or pincers (Gr. *chele*, a claw), epipodite gill-bearing (fig. 1).
10. Ambulatory limb (L. *ambulare*, to walk), epipodite gill-bearing.
The four pair are seen in fig. 1.

ABDOMEN—six pair (see figs. 1-5).

NOTE.—Seven joints of chelæ and ambulatory limbs are named in order as follows (see No. 10)—
1. Coxo'podite (L. *coxa*, the hip) or proximal joint.
2. Basi'podite . . . . } fused together in chela.
3. Ischio'podite (Gr. *ischion*, the hip)
4. Mero'podite (Gr. *meros*, the thigh).
5. Carpo'podite (Gr. *karpos*, wrist).
6. Pro'podite (Gr. *pro*, in front of).
7. Dactylo'podite (Gr. *daktulos*, a finger) or terminal joint.

Six joints of antenna in order (see No. 3)—
Coxo'cerite (Gr. *keras*, a horn).
Basi'cerite articulated with an outer flat plate, scaphocerite.
Ischio'cerite.
Mero'cerite.
Carpo'cerite.
Fla'cerite, the long many-jointed feeler.

Fig 1 Longitudinal Horizontal Section (Female)

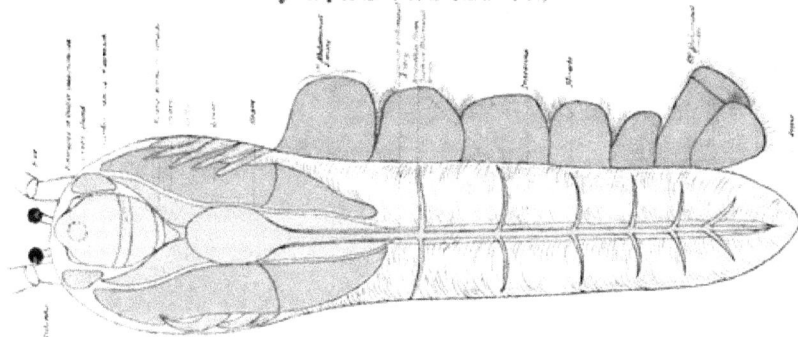

Fig 2 Longitudinal Vertical Section Male

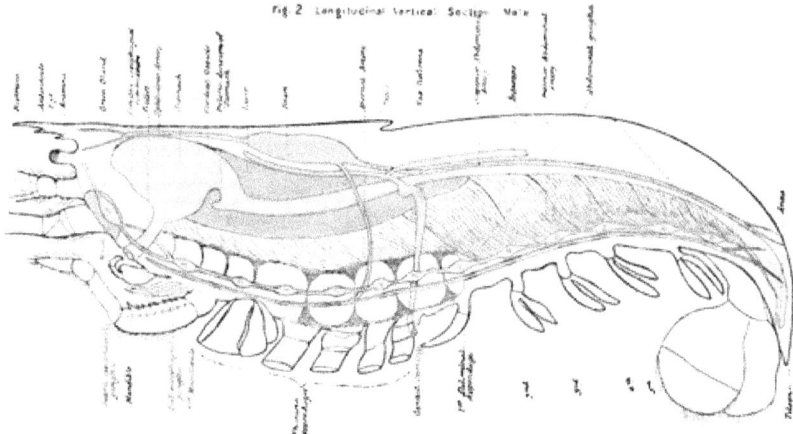

Fig 3 FRESH-WATER CRAYFISH (ASTACUS FLUVIATILIS)
(Female)

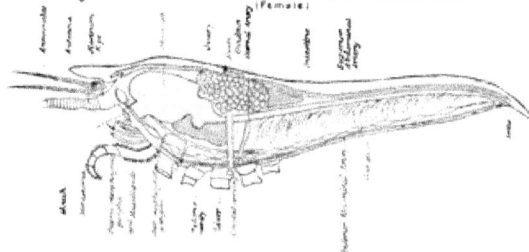

PLATE XIII.

LOBSTER AND CRAYFISH—*continued.*

GENERAL ARRANGEMENT OF INTERNAL ORGANS—
  FIGS. 1, 2, 3. BODY IN SECTIONAL PLAN AND ELEVATION—

ALIMENTARY SYSTEM
- Mouth.
- Gullet.
- Stomach, with its cardiac or anterior end (Gr. *kardia*, the heart), and its pyloric or posterior end (Gr. *pyloros*, a gatekeeper) leading into
- Intestine ending in
- Anus.
- Liver made up of two symmetrical halves.

CIRCULATORY SYSTEM
- Heart.
- Arteries—Sternal, superior abdominal, and inferior abdominal.

RESPIRATORY SYSTEM—Branchiæ (Gr. gills), twenty on each side in Lobster, eighteen in Crayfish.

RENAL SYSTEM—Green glands situated at the base of antennæ.

NERVOUS SYSTEM
- Supra-œsophageal ganglia.
- Circum-œsophageal commissures.
- Sub-œsophageal ganglia.
- Chain of eleven ganglia.

REPRODUCTIVE SYSTEM
- Testes with their vasa deferentia opening on the base of last thoracic appendages (fig. 2).
- Ovaries with their oviducts opening on the base of last thoracic appendages but two (fig. 3).

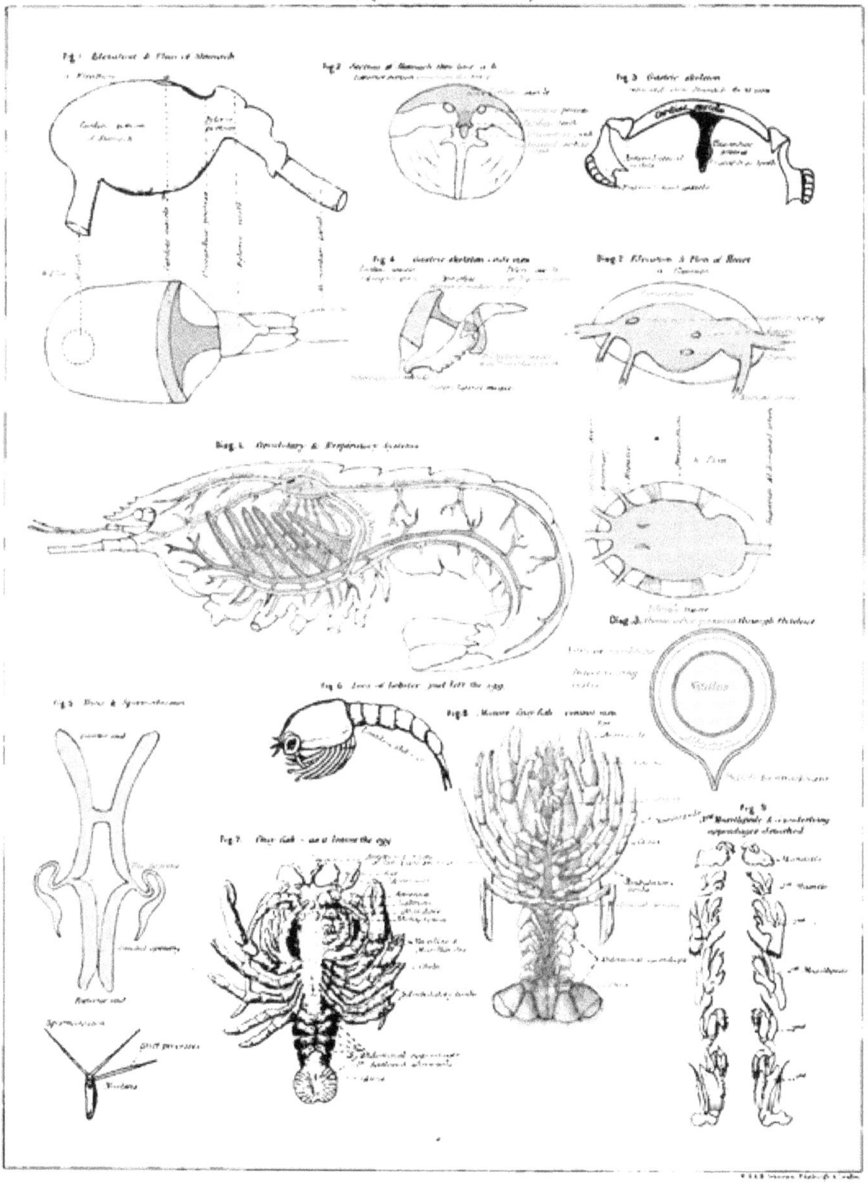
Fig. 1 Elevation & Plan of Stomach
Fig. 2
Fig. 3 Gastric skeleton
Fig. 4 Gastric skeleton
Diag. 2 Elevation & Plan of Heart
Diag. 1 Circulatory & Respiratory Systems
Diag. 3
Fig. 5
Fig. 6 Larva of lobster just left the egg
Fig. 7
Fig. 8
Fig. 9

PLATE XIV.

LOBSTER AND CRAYFISH—*continued.*

ALIMENTARY SYSTEM—

  FIG. 1. STOMACH in Elevation and Plan—

    REGIONS { Anterior or cardiac.

             { Posterior or pyloric, the anterior part of which is the prepyloric.

                  { Cardiac region—cardiac ossicle { Transverse piece.

    SKELETON   {   { Urocardiac process, a median prolongation.

              { Prepyloric region—median prepyloric ossicle (green).

              { Pyloric region—transverse pyloric ossicle.

  FIGS. 2, 3, 4. DETAILED STRUCTURE OF GASTRIC SKELETON—

    Ossicles—

        Cardiac, with urocardiac process.

        Prepyloric (fig. 4).

        Pyloric (fig. 4).

        Lateral   { Anterior pair (figs. 3 and 4).

                 { Posterior pair.

    Teeth of—

        Lateral posterior ossicles.

        Prepyloric ossicle—a single median tooth.

CIRCULATORY AND RESPIRATORY SYSTEMS—

  DIAG. 1. CIRCULATORY AND RESPIRATORY ORGANS—

    Heart, rhythmically contractile and systemic—that is, it propels the blood received from the gills

      through the system.

    Pericardium, a cavity surrounding the heart.

    Arteries carrying the blood to—

        Eye, ophthalmic.

        Antenna, antennary.

        Rest of body, sternal with   { Superior abdominal branch.

                                 { Inferior abdominal branch.

    Veins, gather up blood and carry it to gills for aeration.

    Branchio-cardiac canals, carry blood from gills to pericardium.

    Valvular openings, by which the blood in pericardium enters heart.

    Gills, each consisting of a central stem with an ascending blood-vessel on its outer side leading

      from venous sinus, and a descending blood-vessel on its inner side leading to branchio-

      cardiac canals. The stem is beset with fine filaments which repeat the structure of the stem.

  DIAG. 2. ELEVATION AND PLAN OF HEART—

                    { 1 Ophthalmic.

                    { 2 Antennary.

    ARTERIES . . . . { 2 Hepatic (Gr. *hepar, hepatos,* the liver).

                    { 1 Sternal, with its superior abdominal branch.

                    { 2 Superior.

    VALVULAR APERTURES { 2 Lateral.

                    { 2 Inferior.

    Pericardial cavity, so called pericardium.

    Fibrous tissue, two pair of bands holding heart in place.

REPRODUCTIVE SYSTEM—
  FIG. 5. MALE ORGANS detached (*seen in situ* Pl. XIII. fig. 2) —
      Testes, make spermatozoa.
      Vas deferens, tube for conveying spermatozoa out of body.
      Spermatozoon, cilia absent.
  DIAG. 3. OVUM OF CRAYFISH just hatched—
      Outer and inner membranous coats produced at one point into a process for attachment to the
         body of parent.
      Albumen.
      Vitelline membrane.
      Vitellus.
DEVELOPMENT —
  FIG. 6. Young Lobster as it emerges from egg, a zo'ea which passes by metamorphosis into adult form.
  FIG. 7. Young Crayfish as it emerges from egg, essentially similar to adult, no zoea stage.
  FIG. 8. Adult Crayfish showing appendages.
  FIG. 9. Limbs used for masticatory purposes, laid out.

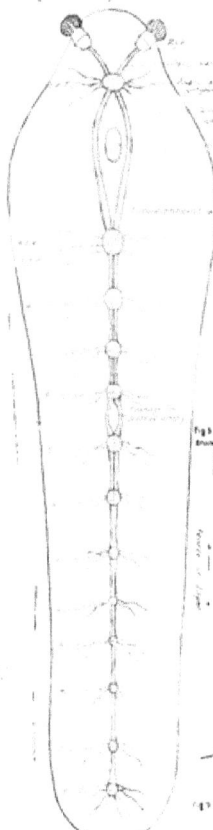

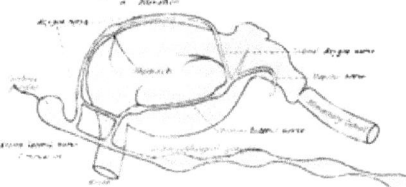

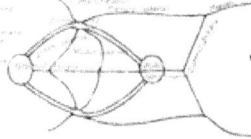

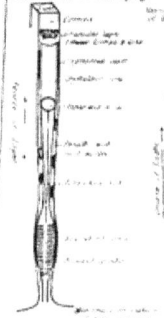

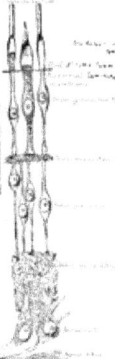

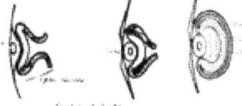

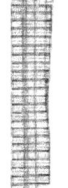

PLATE XV.

LOBSTER—*continued.*

NERVOUS SYSTEM—

FIG. 1. VENTRAL CHAIN of 13 GANGLIA united by commissures—

Cerebral or supra-œsophageal ganglia anterior to gullet, giving off optic nerves.

Circum-œsophageal commissures round gullet.

Sub-œsophageal ganglia posterior to gullet.

5 Remaining thoracic ganglia, united to one another by double nerve-cords.

6 Abdominal ganglia, united to one another by single nerve-cords.

Note.—The numbers attached to ganglia denote the cephalic, thoracic, or abdominal segments to which they belong.

FIG. 2. VISCERAL NERVES in Elevation and Plan—

Nerves arising from—

Cerebral ganglia—Azygos—median, and branching posteriorly to form lateral azygos.

COMMISSURAL GANGLIA
{ Mandibular.
Antero-lateral.
Medio-lateral.
Postero-lateral.

Hepatic formed by the union of postero-lateral and lateral azygos.

SENSORY ORGANS—

FIGS. 3, 4. GENERAL STRUCTURE OF EYE—

Cornea, the transparent cuticle divided into a number of four-sided areas or facets (fig. 4).

Radiating fibres (two are coloured red).

Optic nerve expanding into optic ganglion.

Flexible stalk.

FIG. 5. MINUTE STRUCTURE of one of the elements of the COMPOUND EYE—

Cornea.

NERVOUS ELEMENTS
{ Cone.
Rod.
Spindle.
Nerve-fibril continuous with ganglion.

Investing nervous elements and ganglion.

SHEATH . . . .
{ Outer end continuous with cornea.
Inner end continuous with adjacent sheaths.
Oval nuclei and pigment layers.

DIAG. 2. FORMATION OF THE VERTEBRATE EYE—

a. Optic vesicle, a hollow process of the brain, involution of integument meeting it and pushing it in.

b. Crystalline lens, a detached portion of thickened integument.

c. Retina, the wall of the doubled-up optic vesicle nearest the lens (red).

Choroid, the wall nearest the brain (blue).

Rod and cone layer of retina embedded in the choroid by obliteration of the cavity between.

DIAG. 1. NERVOUS ELEMENTS OF RETINA compared with nervous elements of fig. 5—

Rod, cone, and outer granular layers=cone, rod, and spindle.

Nerve-fibrils continuous with optic ganglion in both.

FIG. 6. Base of antennule cut open to show auditory sac.

FIG. 7. SECTION through AUDITORY SAC—

Auditory opening.

Sac, an involution of the integument lined by hairlike filaments and containing fluid and grains of sand.

Auditory nerve from cerebral ganglia.

FIG. 8. Hairlike filaments magnified.

EXOSKELETON—

Fig. 9. Vertical section of shell or exoskeleton.

The epidermis thrusts off successive layers of its substance, which form a number of delicate laminæ superimposed upon one another, and this is impregnated with salts of lime. The exoskeleton thus formed is cuticular, to be distinguished from cornified epidermis, as nails, composed of modified *cells*, a cellular exoskeleton.

CLASSIFICATION—

Sub-Kingdom—Arthro'poda (Gr. *arthron*, a joint; *pous*, a foot). The body is segmented; limbs jointed; nervous system forms a ring round gullet, followed by a ventral chain of ganglia.

Natural Order—Crustacea (L. *crusta*, a crust), because it breathes by gills, has two pair of antennæ (lesser and greater); walking legs borne by thorax and abdomen.

Genera—Homarus, Astacus.

Common Names—Lobster, Crayfish.

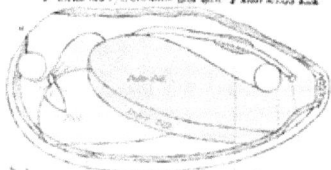

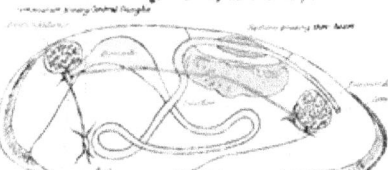

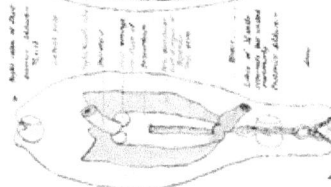

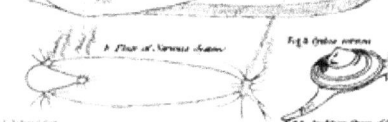

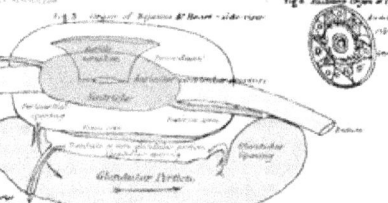

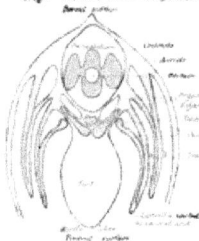

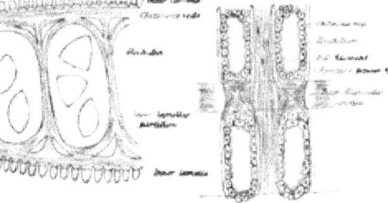

Fig 8.

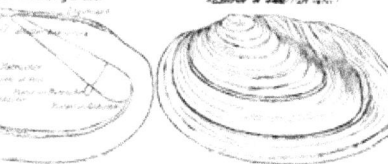

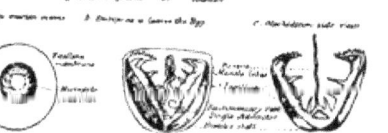

PLATE XVI.

THE FRESH-WATER MUSSEL.

GENERAL STRUCTURE OF BODY—

    FIG. 1, *a*. SIDE VIEW OF ANIMAL when left valve and left mantle-lobe are removed—

        Mouth, anterior.

        Anus, posterior.

        Heart, dorsal.

        Foot, ventral.

        Gills, lateral, inner and outer.

        Labial palps, two on each side of mouth.

        Adductor muscles, anterior and posterior, for closing the shell.

        Right lobe of mantle, lateral.

    FIG. 1, *b*. DORSAL VIEW OF ANIMAL, partly dissected—

        Heart.

        Pericardium.

        Vena cava in floor of pericardium.

        Organ of Bojanus beneath pericardium.

        Intestine entering pericardium.

    DIAG. 1. TRANSVERSE SECTION OF ANIMAL. —

        Mantle-lobes, right and left, lateral extensions of the dorsal integument.

        Outer gill made up of two lamellæ.

        Inner gill made up of two lamellæ.

        Foot, median.

        Pericardium.

        Heart { Ventricle. { Two auricles.

        Intestine piercing ventricle.

        Vena cava.

        Organ of Bojanus, beneath pericardium.

ALIMENTARY AND NERVOUS SYSTEMS—

    FIG. 2, *a*. ALIMENTARY SYSTEM—Mantle and gills removed on left side, and coiled intestine dissected out in foot.

        Mouth, below anterior adductor.

        Gullet.

        Stomach.

        Intestine, with neural flexure.

        Anus, above posterior adductor.

    FIG. 2, *a* and *b*. NERVOUS SYSTEM DISSECTED OUT—

        Cerebral or cephalic ganglia, two at base of labial palps.

        Pedal ganglia, two united and embedded in foot.

        Parieto-splanchnic ganglia (L. *parietes*, walls; Gr. *splanchna*, the entrails), beneath posterior adductor.

        Commissures uniting pedal and parieto-splanchnic with cerebral ganglia.

SENSE ORGANS—

    FIG. 3. Cyclas cornea, a fresh-water form belonging to the same natural order as Anodon, in the foot of which the auditory organ can be conveniently examined under the microscope.

    FIG. 4. AUDITORY ORGAN OF CYCLAS—

        Auditory sac lined with ciliated cells and containing fluid and an otolith in the centre.

        Auditory nerve from pedal ganglion (not shown).

CIRCULATORY AND RENAL SYSTEMS—

    FIG. 5. THE ORGAN OF BOJANUS dissected from left side, left auricle turned up—

        Heart (Systemic) { Auricles receiving blood from gills. { Ventricle with anterior aorta and posterior aorta distributing blood to the body.

Vena cava receiving the blood of the body which passes through the organ of Bojanus to the gills.

ORGAN OF BOJANUS { Transparent non-glandular portion or vestibule communicating with exterior and with the

Brownish glandular portion communicating with pericardium by two oral openings (see fig. 1, b).

RESPIRATORY SYSTEM—

FIG. 6, a. GENERAL STRUCTURE OF GILL, section through line ab in diagram 1—

Inner and outer lamellæ.

Partitions between lamellæ—interlamellar partitions.

Pairs of chitinous rods in the parallel and vertical gill-filaments, indicated by pairs of dots.

FIG. 6, b. MINUTE STRUCTURE OF GILL, section of lamella parallel to surface in region of chitinous rods—

Gill-filament strengthened by pair of chitinous rods.

Openings between filaments furnished with ciliated epithelium.

Partitions between filaments, interfilamentar, consisting of horizontal and obliquely crossed tubes.

MUSCULAR SYSTEM—

FIG. 7. MUSCLES—

Anterior and posterior adductors, adducting or bringing together the valves.

Protractor of foot.

Anterior retractor of foot.

Posterior retractor of foot.

Smaller retractors arising near umbo, impressions only shown (fig. 8, a).

ENDOSKELETON—

FIG. 8, b. EXTERIOR OF SHELL—

Rounded anterior end, tapering posterior end.

Umbo or beak on dorsal surface of each valve towards anterior end.

Concentric lines of growth.

Elastic ligament behind umbones, binding the two valves together, and tending to open the valves. The hinge-line is without interlocking processes or teeth, hence the name Anodon (Gr. a, without ; odous, odontos, a tooth).

FIG. 8, a. INTERIOR OF SHELL—

Pallial impression indicating attachment of muscular ventral edge of mantle to shell.

Anterior and posterior adductor impressions.

Successive adductor impressions, extending from cavity of umbo to each adductor muscle, and indicating the travelling downwards of adductor muscles.

HISTOLOGY—

FIG. 9, a. Liver invests stomach, and consists of blind tubes lined with epithelial cells.

b. Muscle composed of elongated nucleated cells resembling those of smooth muscle in form (Pl. XXIV. fig. 7), but having the structure of striped muscle.

c. Blood-corpuscles, colourless, nucleated, and amœboid.

DEVELOPMENT—

FIG. 10, a. Ripe ovum with its vitelline membrane forming a short tube at one point with an opening or micropyle.

b, c. Embryo when hatched or Glochidium—b enclosed in vitelline membrane, c escaped from it.

DIFFERENCES FROM ADULT { Valves of shell triangular (see fig. 6), united at base and incurved at apex.

Single adductor muscle.

Byssus or beard coming off from foot.

CLASSIFICATION—

Sub-Kingdom—Mollusca (L. mollis, soft). The body is soft and unsegmented ; possesses a shell, and three pair of nervous ganglia.

Natural Order—Lamellibranchiata (L. lamella, a plate ; Gr. branchia, a gill), because it has a bivalve shell ; a two-lobed mantle ; plate-like gills ; and no distinct head.

Genus—Anodonta (Gr. a, without ; odous, odontos, a tooth).

Common Name—Freshwater Mussel.

Fig.1. Helix pomatia

Fig.3. Longitudinal Vertical section

Fig.5. Buccal mass in side view

Fig.2. Shell front view

Fig.6. Horny upper jaw

Diag.1. Long.l Ent. section

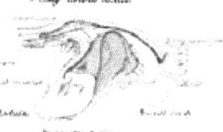

1. Long.l Vertical section

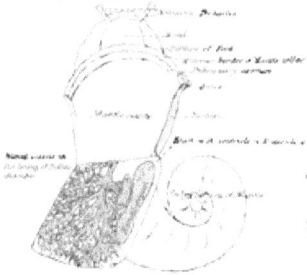

Fig.4. Dorsal view with the upper surface of mantle turned back

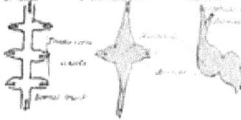

Diag.2. Circulatory System

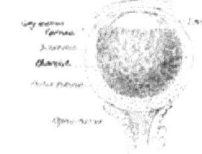

Fig.8. Nasal corpuscles

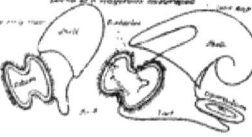

Diag.3. Larva of a oviparous developed

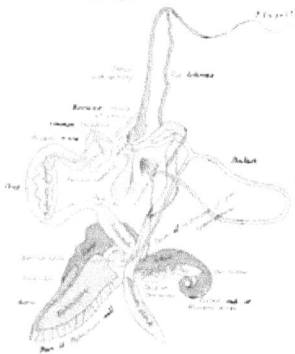

Fig.7. Generative & other organs of Helix aspersa

Fig.10. Blind end of Follicle of Testicles

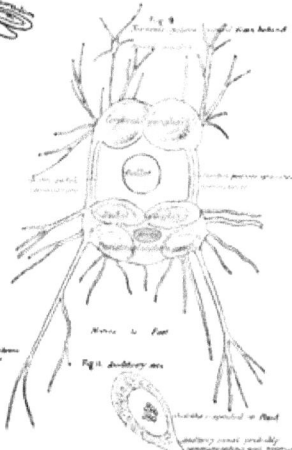

Fig.9. Nervous system spread from behind

Fig.11. Auditory sac

W. & A. K. Johnston, Edinburgh & London.

PLATE XVII.

THE EDIBLE SNAIL.

EXTERNAL CHARACTERS—

    FIG. 1. THE SNAIL protruded from its shell—

        HEAD bearing { Pair of tentacles or eye-stalks with eyes.
                      { Pair of tentacles without eyes.

        Foot flattened out ventrally, hence the name Gasteropod (Gr. *gaster*, the belly ; *pous*, a foot).

        Shell univalve and spiral.

    FIG. 2. SHELL—

        Body-whorl, the last and largest whorl with the mouth.

        Spire, the rest of the whorls.

        Five brown bands running in the direction of the spire.

        Lines of growth running in a longitudinal direction from apex (shown in fig. 1).

GENERAL STRUCTURE OF BODY—

    FIG. 3. SECTION OF BODY, shell and viscera removed—

        Parts of body—foot, mantle, visceral sac, pulmonary chamber.

        BUCCAL CAVITY { Roof with horny jaw.
                     { Floor with odontophore (Gr. *odous*, *odontos*, a tooth ; *phero*, I bear).

        Œsophagus

        Rectum seen in section.

        Nervous ganglia seen in section above and below gullet.

        Columellar muscle attaching body to shell.

    FIG. 4. COMMON SNAIL with shell removed and covering of pulmonary chamber turned back —

        Heart consisting of auricle and ventricle.

        Blood-vessels ramifying in wall of pulmonary chamber.

        Renal organ or kidney for getting rid of nitrogenous waste.

        Pulmonary aperture leading into the modified mantle-cavity or pulmonary chamber, with anus
            beside it.

ALIMENTARY SYSTEM—

    FIG. 5 *a*. BUCCAL MASS removed from body—

        Protractor and retractor muscles.

        Œsophagus and duct of salivary gland leading from it.

    FIG. 5 *b*, and DIAG. 1. ODONTOPHORE IN SECTION—

        Skeleton formed of cartilage (blue).

        Sub-radular membrane with its muscles (yellow).

        Radula (L. a scraper), the surface of sub-radular membrane beset with cuticular teeth (red).

    FIG. 6 —

        a. Horny upper jaw detached.

        b. Teeth of radula arranged in transverse rows.

    FIG. 7. DISSECTION FROM DORSAL SURFACE, with organs gently separated and laid out—

                       { Buccal mass.
                        | Gullet dilating into crop.

        ALIMENTARY SYSTEM .   { Salivary gland embracing crop.

                        | Stomach, with a pyloric caecum near liver.

                        | Liver, with coiled intestine embedded in it.

        CIRCULATORY SYSTEM . { Ventricle (auricle not shown).
                         { Aorta.

        RESPIRATORY SYSTEM .   Pulmonary chamber, with blood-vessels on wall.

        RENAL ORGAN . . . Nephridium (Gr. *nephros*, kidney) or kidney for getting rid of
                              nitrogenous waste.

E

REPRODUCTIVE ORGANS
{
Ovo-testis or hermaphrodite gland embedded in liver, consisting of tubes in which ova and spermatozoa are developed.
  The blind end of one of the tubes with its contained ova and spermatozoa shown in fig. 12.
Duct of ovo-testis.
Albumen-gland forming an albuminous secretion.
Vas deferens or duct for conveying spermatozoa, opening into penis.
Oviduct for conveying ova, ending in vagina.
Spermatheca or receptaculum seminis (L. receptacle of the semen) opening into vagina.
Penis with long flagellum (L. a whip), an eversible involution of the integument.
Dart-sac eversible, with pointed dart } peculiar to Snail family.
Mucous glands . . . . }
}

CIRCULATORY SYSTEM—

  DIAG. 2. COMPARATIVE VIEW OF CENTRES OF CIRCULATION in—
    a. Worm—Dorsal trunk with transverse vessels discharging into it.
    b. Anodon—Dorsal trunk dilated—the ventricle, and transverse vessels reduced to a pair forming the two auricles.
    c. Snail—Dorsal trunk bent upon itself—the ventricle sending blood to anterior end of body by cephalic artery, and to posterior end by abdominal artery. Transverse vessels reduced to one, the right, forming the auricle.
  FIG. 8. COLOURLESS CORPUSCLES OF THE BLOOD.

NERVOUS SYSTEM AND SENSE ORGANS—

  FIG. 9. NERVOUS SYSTEM forming a ring round gullet—
    Cerebral or supra-œsophageal ganglia.
    Sub-œsophageal ganglia { Pedal, anterior and united with cerebral by commissures.
                           { Parieto-splanchnic united with cerebral by commissures.
  FIG. 10. EYES, a pair, placed at end of tentacles—
    Sclerotic (Gr. skleros, hard) passing into a cuticular cornea.
    Choroid, the pigmented layer.
    Optic nerve expanding into an outer retina, the fibres of which pass through the choroid to form an inner retina with rods and cones nearest the light.
    Vitreous humour (not shown).
    Lens.
    Cornea with a conjunctiva on its outer surface.
  FIG. 11. ORGANS OF HEARING, a pair close to pedal ganglia—
    Auditory canal.
    Sac containing fluid and otoliths.
    Auditory nerve from cerebral ganglia (not shown).

DEVELOPMENT—

  DIAG. 3. EARLY STAGES OF DEVELOPMENT OF A VELIGEROUS GASTEROPOD, no evident velum in Snail—
    Ciliated velum, an expansion of the integument about the head.
    Foot developing, with operculum (L. a lid) upon it.
    Shell external.

CLASSIFICATION—

    Sub-Kingdom—Mollusca.
    Natural Order—Odonto'phora, because it has a distinct head; and an Odontophore.
    Genus—Helix (Gr. a spiral), from the spiral form of the univalve shell.
    Common Name—Snail.

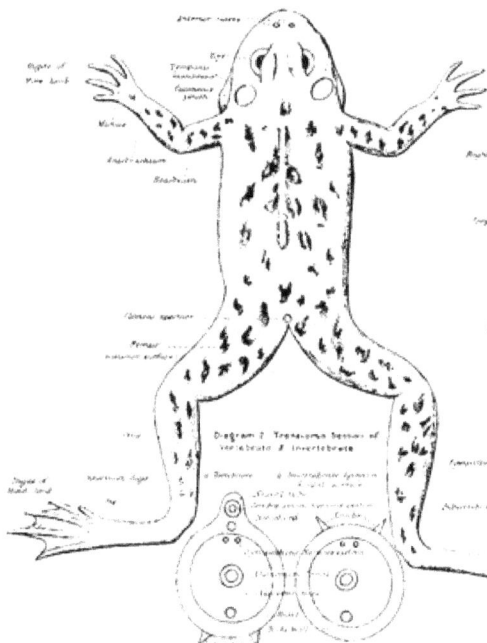

Fig. 1. Extended Frog, dorsal aspect

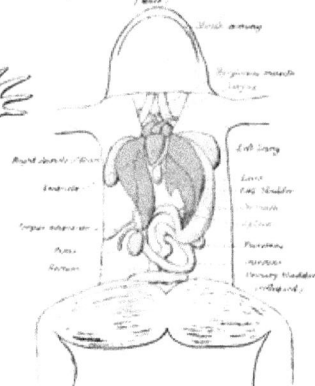

Fig. 2. Dissection from the ventral side. Male

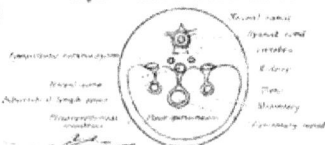

Diagram 1. Transverse Section of Abdomen.

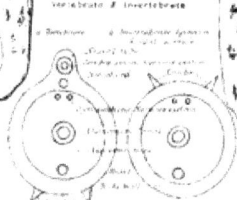

Diagram 2. Transverse Section of Vertebrate & Invertebrate

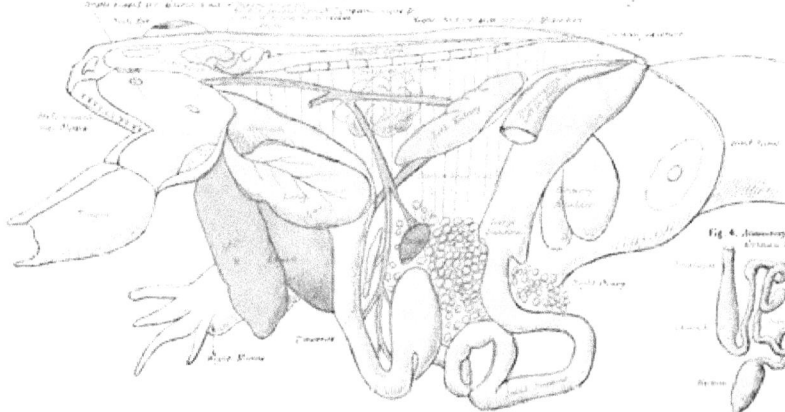

Fig. 3. Longitudinal vertical section with the parts laid out

Fig. 4. Alimentary canal of Rana

PLATE XVIII.

THE FROG.

EXTERNAL CHARACTERS—

    FIG. 1. FROG with Limbs extended—

        Anterior nares or external nares (L. *nares*, the nostrils).

        Eye.

        Tympanic membrane or membrana tympani (L. *tympanum*, a drum).

        Cutaneous pouch (L. *cutis*, the skin).

        Cloacal aperture (L. *cloaca*, a sewer).

        FORE-LIMB
              Brachium (L. the arm).
              Antebrachium (L. *ante*, before).
              Manus (L. the hand).
              Four digits (L. *digitus*, the finger or toe).

        HIND-LIMB
              Femur (L. the thigh).
              Crus (L. the leg).
              Pes (L. the foot).
              Five digits.

GENERAL DISPOSITION OF INTERNAL ORGANS—

    FIG. 2. DISSECTION from the Ventral Surface to show VISCERA, Thoracic and Abdominal—

        HEART
              Ventricle.
              Two auricles.

        Lungs, right and left.

        Stomach and intestine.

        Liver with gall-bladder, pancreas, and spleen.

        Urinary bladder.

        Corpus adiposum (L. fatty body), finger-like yellow processes.

        Testis, only one shown.

    DIAG. 1. TRANSVERSE SECTION THROUGH ABDOMEN—

        NEURAL CANAL containing . . . . Spinal cord.

        PLEUROPERITONEAL CAVITY =
        THORACIC CAVITY lined by the pleura,
        and ABDOMINAL CAVITY lined by the
        peritoneum in Man.

              Lining membrane or pleuroperitoneal membrane (Gr. *pleuron*, a rib; *peri*, around; *teino*, I stretch).

              Alimentary canal suspended by two layers of the membrane coming together in the middle line—the mesentery (Gr. *mesos*, middle; *enteron*, intestine).

              Testes suspended in the same way by the mesorchium (Gr. *orchis*, a testicle).

              Kidneys held in place by the membrane covering their ventral faces.

              Sympathetic nervous system, two gangliated cords contained in triangular space formed by the layers of membrane converging to form mesentery.

              Dorsal aorta.

    DIAG. 2. COMPARISON OF A TRANSVERSE SECTION OF A VERTEBRATE (FROG) AND AN INVERTEBRATE (LOBSTER)—

        Invertebrate—
             Visceral tube only.

        Vertebrate—
             Visceral tube.
             Neural tube.
             Notochord (Gr. *notos*, the back; *chorde*, a string), the primitive axial column, separating the two tubes.

        Limbs on neural or nerve side of body.   Limbs on haemal or heart side of body.

Fig. 3. THE LIMBS on the left side are removed, together with the left walls of the cerebro-spinal, thoraco-abdominal, and buccal cavities. The alimentary canal is laid out to display it to advantage :—

ALIMENTARY SYSTEM	Mouth with posterior nostril, and Eustachian recess continuous with tympanic cavity.
	Tongue turned forward to show its attachment.
	Teeth in upper jaw and on palate.
	Stomach.
	Small intestine succeeding stomach.
	Large intestine terminating in cloaca.
	Liver lobed.
	Pancreas or "sweetbread," pale coloured, near pyloric portion of stomach.
	Spleen, red, near the commencement of twisted portion of intestine.
CIRCULATORY SYSTEM	Dorsal aorta.
	Inferior vena cava.
RESPIRATORY SYSTEM	Glottis, a slit in floor of pharynx leading into lungs.
	Left lung.
•	Right ovary.
RENAL AND REPRODUCTIVE SYSTEMS	Oviduct, anterior coiled portion of right and terminal dilated portion of left (see Pl. XXII. fig. 8).
	Left kidney with ureter.
	Urinary bladder, bilobed.
NERVOUS SYSTEM	Brain and spinal cord.
SKELETON	Vertebral column enclosing spinal cord, and Skull enclosing brain.

Fig. 4. ALIMENTARY CANAL removed from body:—
Œsophagus or gullet communicating with pharynx.

STOMACH	Cardiac or anterior portion.
	Pyloric portion leading into intestine.
SMALL INTESTINE	Duodenum forming a loop with the stomach.
	Ileum, the twisted portion (Gr. *eilein*, to twist).
LARGE INTESTINE	Colon, the dilated portion into which the ileum opens.
	Rectum (L. the seat) opening into cloaca.

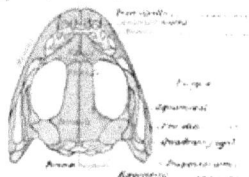

Fig. 1. Skull dorsal view

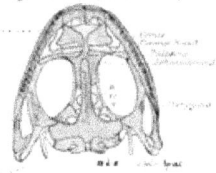

Fig. 2. Skull ventral view

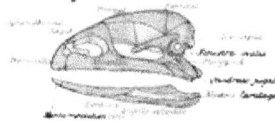

Fig. 3. Skull lateral view

Fig. 4. Skull posterior view

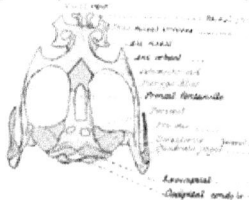

Fig. 5. Cartilaginous skull dorsal view

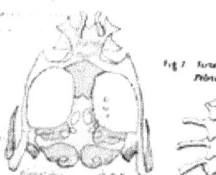

Fig. 6. Cartilaginous skull ventral view

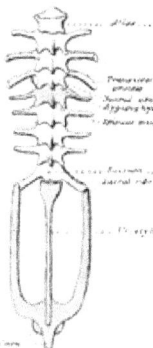

Fig. 7. Vertebral column & Pelvic Girdle dorsal aspect

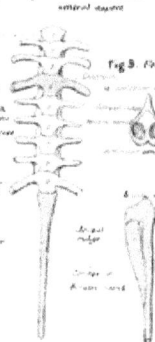

Fig. 8. Vertebral column ventral aspect

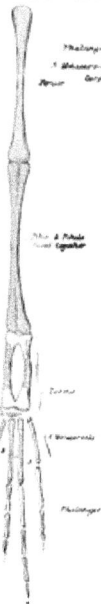

Fig. 9. Urostyle

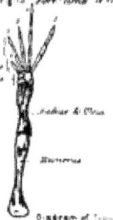

Fig. 13. Fore limb of Common Frog

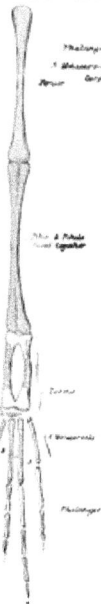

Fig. 14. Hind limb of Edible Frog

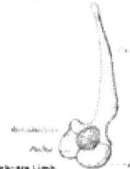

Fig. 10. Pelvis side view

Diagram of Typical Vertebrate Limb

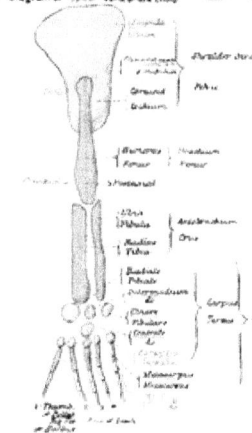

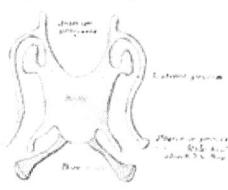

Fig. 11. Hyoid bone or cartilage - ventral view

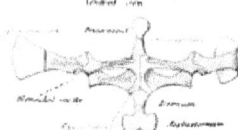

Fig. 12. Sternum & Shoulder girdle ventral view

PLATE XIX.

THE FROG—*continued.*

SKELETON.

⁎ The colours in left-hand corner of Plate refer only to Skull.

THE BONY SKULL:—

  FIG. 1. DORSAL VIEW:—

   Exoccipitals (L. *ex*, out; *occiput*, the back of the head).

   Pro-otics (Gr. *pro*, in front of ; *ous, otos*, the ear).

   Parietals (L. *paries*, a wall) . . . } united in adult.
   Frontals (L. *frons*, the forehead) }

   Nasals.

   Premaxillæ (L. *præ*, before ; *maxilla*, the upper jaw).

  FIG. 2. VENTRAL VIEW, lower jaw removed—

   Parasphenoid (Gr. *sphen*, a wedge).

   Sphenethmoid or girdle-bone.

   Vomers with teeth.

   Premaxillæ with teeth.

   Pterygoids (Gr. *pteron*, a wing).

   Palatines, slender palate bones.

  FIG. 3. SIDE VIEW—

   Squamosals.

   Quadrato-jugals.

   Maxillæ with teeth.

   Premaxillæ with teeth.

   Mandible or lower jaw, consisting of two rami (L. *ramus*, a branch) without teeth.

   RAMUS { Meckel's cartilage forming the core.
   { Angulo-splenial . . } investing Meckel's cartilage.
   { Dentary without teeth }
   { Mento-Meckelian bone (L. *mentum*, the chin), the ossified tip of Meckel's cartilage.

  FIG. 4. POSTERIOR VIEW—

   Exoccipitals with condyles (Gr. *kondulos*, a knuckle) for articulation with vertebral column.

   Foramen magnum (L. great opening), through which spinal cord passes into brain.

THE CARTILAGINOUS SKULL—

  FIG. 5. DORSAL VIEW—

   Sphenethmoid bone, replacing cartilage and partly covered by the frontals (see fig. 1).

   Nasal roof covered by nasals.

   Fontanelles, membranous portions.

  FIG. 6. VENTRAL VIEW—

   Sphenethmoid bone.

   Nasal floor anterior to sphenethmoid covered by vomers.

   Floor posterior to sphenethmoid from the exoccipitals covered by the parasphenoid, which partly overlaps sphenethmoid.

   Pterygoid bar, replaced by pterygoid and palatine bones (see fig. 2).

  FIGS. 5, 6. MANDIBULAR SUSPENSORIUM, connecting lower jaw with skull—

   Posterior end articulating with Meckel's cartilage.

   Anterior end dividing { Dorsal process or crus attached to outer wall of skull.
   into . . . . . { Ventral process or crus continuous with pterygoid bar.

   Note.—Two kinds of bone are distinguished in the skull according to their mode of origin—
   1. Cartilage bones (red), as the name denotes, are first modelled in cartilage.
   2. Membrane or splint bones (blue) are those not so preformed in cartilage.

Figs. 7, 8, 9. The Vertebral Column or Backbone—9 bony segments or vertebræ and a bony prolongation or urostyle (Gr. *oura*, a tail)—

Vertebra . . . . { Body or centrum.
{ Neural arch { Neural spine or spinous process.
{ Transverse processes.
{ Zygapophyses (Gr. *zygos*, an articulation).

Atlas or 1st vertebra with which the two occipital condyles of the skull articulate.

Sacrum or 9th vertebra with which the pelvic girdle articulates.

Urostyle or Coccyx { Thickened anterior end with two concavities into which the two convexities of the sacrum fit (fig. 9, *a*).
{ Sciatic nerve, the nerve of the leg, passing out from neural canal by a small opening (rod).

Fig. 10. Pelvic Arch, side view—

Pelvic Arch or Hip-Girdle . . . . { Acetabulum, the socket into which the head of the thigh-bone or femur fits.
{ Ilium or haunch-bone articulating with sacrum.
{ Ischium, a posterior rounded bone.
{ Pubis, a ventral wedge between ilium and ischium.
{ Triradiate junction of the three bones in the acetabulum.

Fig. 11. Hyoid—

Body.

Processes or Cornua (L. horns) . . . { Anterior attached to skull (see fig. 2).
{ Lateral.
{ Posterior.
{ Thyro-hyals, sometimes called posterior cornua.

Fig. 12. Sternum and Shoulder-Girdle—

Sternum or Breast-Bone . . . . { Anterior piece—Omo-sternum (Gr. *omos*, the shoulder).
{ Median piece—Sternum proper.
{ Posterior piece—Xiphi-sternum (Gr. *xiphos*, a sword).

Pectoral Arch or Shoulder-Girdle { Glenoidal cavity, the socket into which the head of the humerus fits.
{ Dorsal portion—Scapula or shoulder-blade, and Supra-scapula.
{ Ventral portions { Coracoids.
{ Clavicle or collar-bone.

Fig. 13. Right Fore-Limb, dorsal surface—

Humerus.

Radius and ulna united.

Carpals or wrist-bones.

Five digits consisting of metacarpals and phalanges (first digit rudimentary—Pollex, L. thumb).

Fig. 14. Left Hind-Limb, dorsal surface—

Femur or thigh-bone.

Tibia and fibula united.

Tarsals with elongated astragalus and calcaneum.

Five digits consisting of metatarsals and phalanges.

Calcar (L. a spur), a horny projection at base of first digit or hallux (L. *hallex*, the big toe).

Diagram. The corresponding Bones in the Fore and Hind Limbs with their respective Arches—

The axis (an imaginary line passing through the middle of the limb to the end of the third digit) divides the limb into a proaxial and a postaxial portion.

Carpus or tarsus consists of two rows of bones with a centrale between, and the following are thus named in human anatomy:—

Radiale	= Scaphoid.	Tibiale	} = Astra'galus.
Intermedium	= Lunar.	Intermedium	
Ulnare	= Cu'neiform.	Fibulare	= Calca'neum.
Centrale, not represented.		Centrale	= Navicula're.

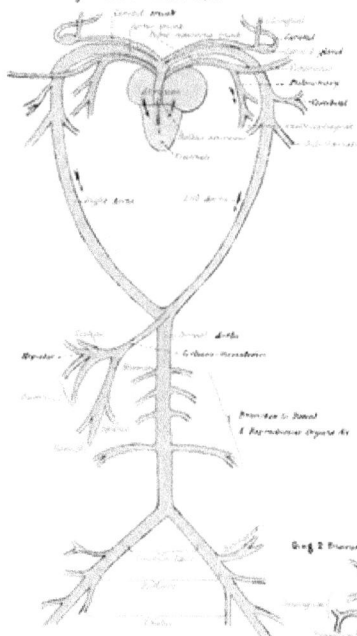

Fig. 1. *Arteries ventral aspect*

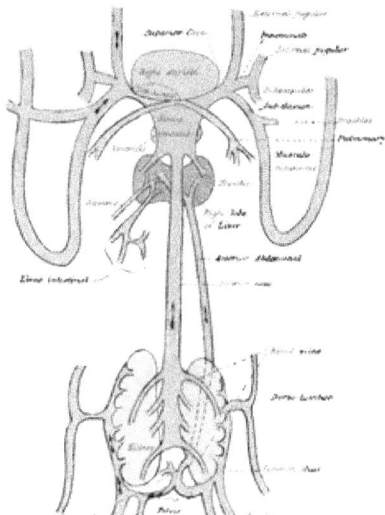

Fig. 2. *Veins dorsal aspect*

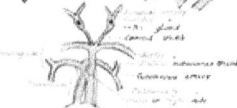

Fig. 2. *Thorax venous land open.*

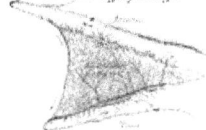

Fig. 3. *Web of foot slightly enlarged*

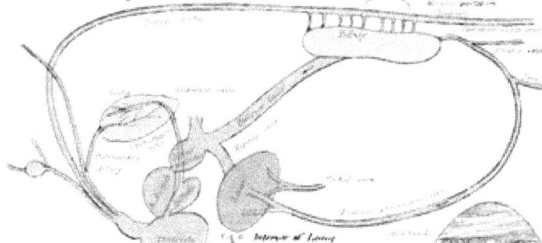

Fig. 3. *General scheme of Circulation.*

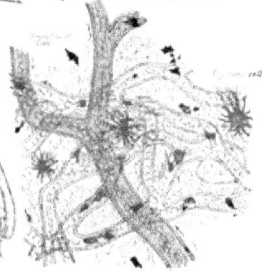

Fig. 4. *Portion of Capillary network*

Fig. 5. *Cartilages of Larynx & Trachea*

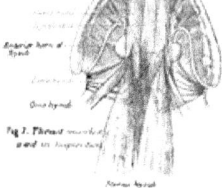

Fig. 7. *Throat muscles & used in respiration.*

PLATE XX.

THE FROG—*continued.*

CIRCULATORY SYSTEM—

FIG. 1. ARTERIES—

CAROTID TRUNK OR AN-
TERIOR AORTIC ARCH
- Lingual artery (L. *lingua*, the tongue) to tongue.
- Carotid gland.
- Carotid artery to head by way of ear (Gr. *kara*, the head; *ous*, the ear).

AORTIC TRUNK OR
MIDDLE AORTIC
ARCH . . . . .
- Vertebral artery to vertebral column.
- Sub-clavian artery (L. *sub*, under; *clavicula*, collar-bone) to forelimb.
- Œsophageal artery to gullet.
- Cœliac artery { Hepatic to liver.
  (Gr. *koilia*, the belly) { Gastric to stomach.
- Mesenteric artery { Splenic to spleen.
  { Hæmal to intestine (not named).
- Dorsal aorta, giving off branches to various organs.
- Common iliac arteries formed by the forking of the aorta in the neighbourhood of the ilium, and giving off hypogastric branches to the bladder and lower parts of the belly.
- Femoral and sciatic arteries, a continuation of the common iliac down the thigh.

PULMO-CUTANEOUS
TRUNK OR POS-
TERIOR AORTIC
ARCH . . . . .
- Pulmonary artery to lung (L. *pulmo*, a lung).
- Cutaneous artery to the skin of the back (L. *cutis*, the skin).

FIG. 2. VEINS—

SUPERIOR VENA CAVA,
FORMED BY . . .
- Innominate, formed by { Internal jugular.
  { Sub-scapular.
- Sub-clavian, formed by { Musculo-cutaneous.
  { Brachial.
- External jugular.

INFERIOR VENA CAVA,
FORMED BY . . . .
- Renal.
- Genital (not shown).
- Hepatic.

COMMON ILIAC or RENAL AFFERENT VEIN formed by the dorsal ends of the pelvic vein, which is formed by the femoral and sciatic veins. Dorso-lumbar vein opens into common iliac.

ANTERIOR ABDOMINAL VEIN formed by the ventral ends of the pelvic vein.

PORTAL VEIN or VENA PORTÆ (L. the vein of the gate—of the liver) formed by { Gastric.
{ Lieno-intestinal (L. *lien*, the spleen).

COMMON PULMONARY VEIN formed by the veins of the right and left lungs.

DIAGRAM I. THE HEART, with the principal vessels distributing and returning the blood—

HEART . . . .
- Sinus venosus (L. venous sinus) receiving superior and inferior venæ cavæ.
- Right auricle with sinus venosus opening into it.
- Left auricle receiving common pulmonary vein.
- Ventricle leading into truncus arteriosus (L. arterial trunk).

PRINCIPAL ARTERIAL TRUNKS
{ Carotid supplying the parts about the head, including the brain.
Pulmo-cutaneous supplying the lungs and dorsal integument.
Aortic supplying the rest of the body.

PRINCIPAL VENOUS TRUNKS
{ Superior cava returning blood from the head, forelimbs, and dorsal integument chiefly.
Pulmonary veins returning blood from the lungs.
Vena portæ returning blood from the stomach, intestine, spleen and pancreas to liver.
Anterior abdominal returning blood from the urinary bladder and belly-walls to liver.
Inferior cava returning blood from the hind-limbs, kidneys, and liver chiefly.

DIAGRAM II. TRUNCUS ARTERIOSUS laid open to show action of heart—

Pylangium (Gr. *pule*, gate ; *angeion*, a vessel), or receiving part, contains a median longitudinal valve or movable partition attached to the dorsal surface, and a small transverse valve on the right side.

Synangium (Gr. *sun*, together), or distributing terminal part, gives rise to Pulmo-cutaneous, Aortic, and Carotid trunks.

FIGS. 3, 4. CIRCULATION OF THE BLOOD IN THE WEB—

Arteries with flow of blood towards the *smaller* branches.
Capillaries arising from the ultimate branches of the arteries and giving rise to the veins.
Veins with flow of blood from smaller to larger vessels.
Oval blood-corpuscles coursing through the vessels.
Pigment-cells on the surface

RESPIRATORY SYSTEM—

FIGS. 5, 6. STRUCTURE AND FRAMEWORK of the Respiratory Organs—

FIG. 5. Glottis (Gr. *glotta*, the tongue), a longitudinal slit opening into the floor of the back part of the mouth or pharynx (Pl. XVIII. Fig. 3).

Arytenoid cartilages, one on each side of the glottis, movable inwards and outwards.

Laryngo-tracheal cartilage, a ring forming the very short tube common to the two lungs.

FIG. 6. The Lung is a thin-walled, elastic, and transparent bag, the inner surface of which shows shallow depressions produced by infoldings of the wall, and corresponding to the air cells of higher animals.

FIG 7. MUSCLES of the throat for depressing and raising the floor of the mouth—inspiratory muscles.

MUSCLES HAVING THEIR "ORIGIN" IN ANTERIOR PORTION OF HYOID . .
{ Mylo-hyoid (Gr. *mule*, a mill), insertion in rami of mandible.
Genio-hyoid, insertion in symphysis of mandible or chin.
Hyo-glossus (Gr. *glossa*, the tongue), insertion in tongue.
Petro-hyoid, insertion in auditory capsule.

MUSCLES HAVING THEIR "INSERTION" IN POSTERIOR PORTION OF HYOID . .
{ Omo-hyoid (Gr. *omos*, the shoulder), origin in scapula.
Sterno-hyoid, origin in sternum.

NOTE.—The point of attachment comparatively fixed is called the Origin of the Muscle, while the attachment to the part to be moved is called its Insertion.

PLATE XXI.

THE FROG—continued.

Nervous System—

Figs. 1, 2. The Brain or Encephalon (Gr. en, in; kephale, the head)—

Fore-Brain	Olfactory lobes or Rhinencephalon (Gr. rhis, rhinos, the nose) giving off olfactory nerves.
	Cerebral hemispheres or Prosencephalon (Gr. pros, before) completely separated by the great fissure (fig. 3).
	Optic thalami (Gr. thalamos, a bed), one on each side bounding the third ventricle with pineal gland on roof = Thalamencephalon.
Mid-Brain (Yellow)	Optic lobes above and crura cerebri (L. legs of the cerebrum) below = Mesencephalon (Gr. mesos, middle).
Hind-Brain	Cerebellum (L. the little brain), very small = Metencephalon (Gr. meta, behind).
	Medulla oblongata (L. elongated marrow) with the fourth ventricle = Myelencephalon (Gr. myelos, marrow).

Lamina terminalis (L. terminal plate), the anterior wall of the thalamencephalon terminating the axial portion of the brain, the hemispheres being lateral expansions.

Fig. 3. The Cavities of the Brain, so-called Ventricles—

1. Olfactory.
2. Lateral . . . } Aperture of communication, foramen of Munro.
3. Third ventricle }
   Iter a tertio ad quartum ventriculum (L. passage from third to fourth ventricle), with ventricles of optic lobes entering it.
4. Fourth ventricle, continuous with central canal of spinal cord.

Fig. 4. General View of the Brain and Spinal Cord, cerebro-spinal axis—

Brain showing chiasma (Gr. a crossing) of the optic nerves, and optic tracts leading from optic lobes.

Spinal cord or myelon, tapering away to the filum terminale (L. terminal thread).

Diag. 1. Ten pair of Cranial Nerves, ten pair of Spinal Nerves, and ten pair of Sympathetic Ganglia—

Cranial Nerves, 1 to 10 (yellow).

Spinal Nerves (blue)	Spinal 1, hypoglossal (Gr. hupo, under; glossa, a tongue), distributed to tongue.
	,, 2 and 3, forming a brachial plexus (L. brachium, an arm; plexus, a junction), and distributed to fore-limbs.
	,, 4, 5, and 6, distributed to the body-walls.
	,, 7, 8, and 9, forming a lumbo-sacral plexus (L. lumbus, the loin), and distributed to posterior portion of body and hind-limbs; crural to front of limb and sciatic (contraction for ischiatic) to back of it.
	,, 10, distributed to parts about coccyx.

Sympathetic Ganglia (S. 1 to S. 10), with connecting commissures (red).

Diag. 2. Contents of Neural Canal, as seen in a transverse section—

Spinal Cord	Grey matter, a central square with its four corners passing into the posterior (dorsal) and anterior (ventral) roots of the nerve-trunk.
	Central canal lined with epithelium.
	White matter outside grey matter { Posterior fissure (dorsal). { Anterior fissure (ventral).

MEMBRANES LINING CANAL AND INVESTING CORD { Pia mater, a vascular membrane investing cord and continuous with Dura mater lining canal (red).

Arachnoid superficial to pia mater and dura mater, and secreting arachnoid fluid (blue).

FIG. 5 and DIAG. 3. CRANIAL NERVES, and their distribution—

    I. Olfactory (L. *oleo*, I smell) distributed to olfactory sac, as shown in Diag. 1.

    II. Optic distributed to eye (Diag. 3).

    III. Oculo-motor (L. *oculus*, eye; *motor*, mover) distributed to four muscles of eye (Diag. 3).

    IV. Pathetic distributed to superior oblique muscle (Diag. 3).

    V. Trigeminal dilates into Gasserian ganglion giving off—

        V¹. Orbito-nasal or ophthalmic distributed chiefly to the nasal chamber.

        V². Superior maxillary distributed to upper jaw.

        V³. Inferior maxillary or mandibular distributed to lower jaw or mandible.

    VI. Abducens (L. *abduco*, I draw away) distributed to external rectus muscle (Diag. 3).

    VII. Facial or *portio dura* (blue) dividing at Gasserian ganglion into—

        VII¹. Or anterior distributed chiefly to the palate.

        VII². Or posterior dividing into a branch to the hyoid and a branch to mandible by way of tympanic cavity = chorda tympani (L. cord of the drum).

    VIII. Auditory or *portio mollis* distributed to the auditory capsule (Diag. 1).

    IX. Glossopharyngeal (Gr. *glossa*, the tongue; *pharynx*, the throat) distributed to tongue and pharynx (yellow).

    X. Pneumogastric (Gr. *pneumon*, the lungs; *gaster*, the stomach) or Vagus (L. wandering) (red) —

        X¹. Cutaneous branch distributed to dorsal integument.

        X². Cardiac branch distributed to heart.

        X³. Laryngeal branch distributed to larynx.

        X⁴. Pulmonic branch distributed to lungs.

        X⁵. Gastric branch distributed to gullet and stomach.

FIG. 6. NERVES OF HIND-LIMB, bones displaced to show nerves of dorsal surface—

    SCIATIC { Peroneal (Gr. *perone*, the fibula) running beside peroneus muscle.

        { Posterior tibial running beside tibialis posticus muscle.

MUSCULAR SYSTEM—

DIAG. 3. MUSCLES OF EYE.

FIG. 7. SUPERFICIAL MUSCLES OF HIND-LIMB. Frog dissected when laid on back, with dorsal surface of foot uppermost.

	Name.	Origin.	Insertion.
THIGH	Adductores—brevis, magnus, and longus.	Pelvis.	Femur.
	Sartorius.	Pubis.	Crus, inner side of knee-joint.
	Rectus internus major.	Pubis.	Iba.
	Rectus internus minor.	Pelvis.	Do.
	Vastus internus.	Pelvis, near to hip-joint.	Do.
LEG	Gastrocnemius, the bulk of the calf of the leg (Gr. *gaster*, the belly; *kneme*, the leg).	Partly femur, partly crus.	Ending in tendo Achillis.
	Tibialis posticus (L. posterior tibial).	Crus.	Astragalus.
	Peroneus.	Femur.	Calcaneum.
	Tibialis anticus (L. anterior tibial).	Femur.	Astragalus and calcaneum.
	Extensor cruris brevis (L. short extender of the leg).	Femur.	Crus.
	Flexor tarsi anterior (L. anterior bender of the tarsus).	Femur.	Astragalus.

Name.		Origin.	Insertion.
Fig. 8. Deep Muscles on front or ventral surface of thigh—			
Pectin'eus.		Pelvis.	Femur.
Adductor brevis, also seen on surface.			
Semitendinosus.		Pelvis.	Crus.
Vastus internus, also seen on surface.			
Fig. 9. Muscles on back of thigh—for dissection lay out as in Pl. XVIII. fig. 1.			
Triceps femoris (L. *triceps*, having three heads)	Vastus internus. Rectus femoris anticus (not shown). Vastus externus.	Pelvis.	Crus.
Gluteus (Gr. *gloutos*, the buttock).		Pelvis.	Femur.
Pyriformis.		Urostyle.	Femur.
Biceps femoris (L. *biceps*, having two heads).		Pelvis.	Femur.
Semimembranosus.		Pelvis.	Crus and femur, round knee-joint.
Rectus internus, seen also on front.			

PLATE XXII.

THE FROG—*continued.*

SENSE ORGANS—

FIG. 1. EYE OF OX divided—(*a*) Into a right and left half—left half shown.

(*b, c*) Along equator into an anterior and posterior half.

Sclerotic or outer coat passing into transparent cornea in front.

Choroid coat pigmented, anterior end raised into longitudinal plaits—the *ciliary processes*.

Iris (L. a rainbow), anterior to ciliary processes, and connected to sclerotic where it passes into cornea by the *ciliary muscle*.

Lens enclosed in capsule, which is attached to the inner side of the choroid by *suspensory ligament*.

Ciliary muscle dips into folds of ciliary processes above, just as suspensory ligament dips into them below (*b*).

Aqueous humour anterior to lens.

Vitreous humour posterior to lens.

Retina inside choroid.

Optic nerve entering a little to one side of axis by the optic pore.

FIG. 1 *c.* Blood-vessels are seen to enter retina from the spot where optic nerve enters.

FIG. 2. GENERAL VIEW OF RIGHT EAR OF FROG—

Tympanic cavity exposed by removing tympanic membrane.

Three semicircular canals.

Columella auris (L. little column of the ear).

FIG. 3. MEMBRANOUS LABYRINTH OF LEFT EAR—

Semicircular canals, anterior, posterior, and horizontal, each dilated at one end into ampulla (L. ampulla, I swell out), and two ends of vertical canals joining together.

Vestibule...... { Utriculus (L. a little bag), into which semicircular canals open. { Sacculus (L. a small bag).

Cochlea (L. a snail's shell), rudimentary.

FIG. 4. ESSENTIAL PARTS OF HUMAN EAR, natural size—

External ear—Pinna or concha (L. a shell), not shown.

Auditory meatus (L. a canal).

Middle ear {
Tympanic membrane.

Tympanic cavity or tympanum opening by Eustachian tube into pharynx.

Auditory ossicles or ear-bones bridging over cavity { Malleus (L. a hammer). { Incus (L. an anvil). { Stapes (L. a stirrup).

Fenestra ovalis (L. oval window), an oval membrane, to which foot-plate of stapes is attached.

Fenestra rotunda (L. round window), at the base of cochlea.
}

Internal ear or labyrinth {
Semicircular canals, horizontal not shown.

Vestibule into which canals open.

Cochlea, also communicating with vestibule.
}

FIG. 5. AUDITORY OSSICLES OF HUMAN EAR, magnified.

FIG. 6. COLUMELLA AURIS detached (see also fig. 2)—

Stapes or inner end fits into fenestra ovalis.

Extra-stapedial or outer end attached to tympanic membrane.

Renal and Reproductive Organs —

Fig. 7. Male Organs from the ventral surface. The right testis is turned over to show its efferent ducts —

Testes on the ventral side of kidneys.

Vasa efferentia (i. e. afferent vessels), leading to inner side of kidney.

Kidneys in the dorsal part of abdominal cavity.

Duct passing from outer side of kidney to open into cloaca. Genito-urinary canal, because it serves as ureter for the kidney and vas deferens for the testis.

Fig. 8. Female Organs removed from body —

Ovary much folded and distended with ova.

Oviduct distinct from ovary, anterior end opening beside gullet, posterior end in cloaca.

Ureter slender and opening into cloaca, posteriorly to oviduct.

Openings into cloaca — Rectum.

Urinary bladder, on ventral side of rectum independent of ureter.

Oviduct, anterior to opening of ureter.

Ureter.

Figs. 9, 10. Malpighian Capsule of Human Kidney —

Tubule with its rounded dilatation, the Malpighian capsule.

Glomerulus (i. e. a ball), the tuft of looped capillaries formed by afferent vessel from renal artery, and uniting again to form an efferent vessel (vein), which breaks up into capillaries on the wall of the tubule.

Epithelium of capsule, glomerulus, and tubule.

Fig. 11. Malpighian Capsule of Frog's Kidney —

Epithelium lining tubule, with cilia to expel the urine.

Fig. 12. Ovum and Spermatozoon of Common Frog —

Spermatozoon with vibratile tail.

Tadpole or Larval Frog at different Stages.

Figs. 13, 14. External Branchiæ, three on each side of neck.

Suckers, dilatation of its integument secreting a sticky substance.

Horny jaws.

Operculum or gill-cover beginning to form.

Fig. 15. Operculum grown over gills, leaving only a small opening on left side for some time.

Hind-limbs appearing at first as tubercles, fore-limbs hidden by operculum.

Fig. 16. Head of very young Tadpole, magnified —

Visceral clefts, six on each side of neck.

External branchiæ, two on each side of neck (a third pair afterwards developed

PLATE XXIII.

THE FROG—*continued.*

DEVELOPMENT—

    FIG. 1. EGGS, natural size (see Pl. XXII. fig. 12, Egg magnified)—

        a. Ovarian ova.

        b. Laid eggs, surrounded by successive layers of albumen or white of egg secreted by the oviduct and swelling up in water.

    FIG. 2. IMPREGNATED EGG showing successive stages in the process of yelk-division—

        The immediate result of this process is the formation of a morula (*f*), which by the soaking in of fluid into its interior becomes a hollow sphere.

    DIAG. 1. DEVELOPMENT OF TADPOLE—

        a. Blastoderm or germinal membrane { Outer layer or epiblast.
        Middle layer or mesoblast.
        Inner layer or hypoblast (blue).

        Medullary groove, a median longitudinal depression.

        Laminæ dorsales (L. dorsal plates) or medullary folds, the epiblast raised up into folds on each side of medullary groove.

        Notochord or chorda dorsalis, the primitive axial column.

        d. Neural canal formed by the union of the dorsal laminæ, with neural arches in its walls.

        Centra of spinal column invest notochord, which persists both in the centres of the bodies of the vertebræ and in the urostyle.

        f. Spirally-coiled intestine.

        Large muscular tail.

        Chief phases in life of Tadpole shown in Pl. XXII.

    FIG. 3. Perfect Frog, tailless, in natural position.

CLASSIFICATION—

        Sub-Kingdom—Vertebrata, because it possesses a vertebral column ; limbs with an internal skeleton ; and a portal vein with a capillary network at both its ends, receiving the capillaries of the alimentary canal, and distributing to the capillaries of the liver.

        Class—Amphibia (Gr. *amphi*, both ; *bios*, life), because as a Tadpole it has gills, afterwards lungs ; two condyles on the skull for articulation with the vertebral column ; and a cloaca.

        Natural Order—Anou'ra (Gr. *a*, without ; *oura*, a tail), because devoid of tail and gills in adult life.

        Genus—Rana.

        Common Name—Frog.

Comparative Histology of Frog and Man.

    FIGS. 4, 4*a.* BLOOD-CORPUSCLES —

        Red { Frog—large, oval, and nucleated.
        Human—smaller, round, and non-nucleated.

        Colourless, like amœbæ (see Pl. IX. fig. 4).

    FIGS. 5, 5*a.* EPITHELIUM (Gr. *epi*, upon ; *thallo*, I grow) in its principal varieties—

        a. Squamous (L. *squama*, a scale) or scaly.

        b. Columnar or cylindrical.

        c. Ciliated.

        Sphœroidal or glandular (see Pl. XXII. fig. 11).

    FIG. 6. *a, b, c.* CONNECTIVE TISSUE in its two principal varieties—

        WHITE FIBROUS TISSUE { Connective-tissue corpuscles, nucleated cells.
        Matrix, fibrous.

        YELLOW ELASTIC TISSUE, resisting acetic acid.

    FIG. 7 and DIAG. 2. VERTICAL SECTION OF EPIDERMIS OR EPITHELIUM.

    FIG. 8. *a, b.* CARTILAGE OR GRISTLE—

        Cartilage { Matrix, granular.
        Cartilage cells, nucleated.

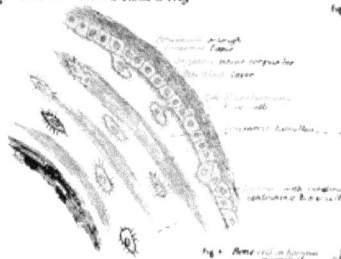

Fig 1 *Transverse section of Femur of Frog*

Fig 2 *Transverse section of compact bone of human Femur*

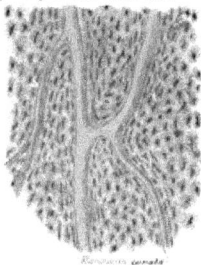

Fig 3 *Long¹ section of Human Femur*

Fig 4 *Bone cell in human*

Fig 5
a *striped muscle of Frog*
b *The same treated with acetic acid*

Fig 6 *Striped human muscle Fibre*

Fig 7 *Smooth muscular fibre*

Fig 8
a *Nerve fibre taken from back of Frog*
b *Human nerve fibre*

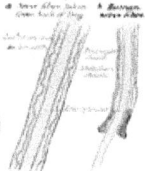

Fig 9 *Nerve cells*

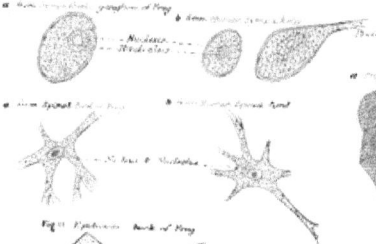

Fig 10 *Structure of Liver*
a *Frog*
b *Human*

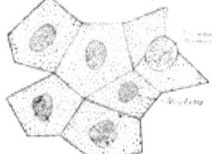

Fig 11 *Epithelium back of Frog*

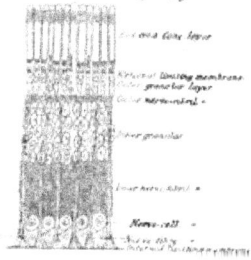

Fig 13 *Nervous & connective elements of Eye of Frog*

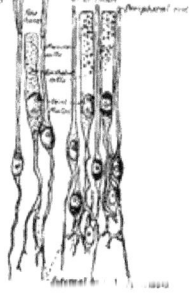

Fig 14 *Cells forming Nerve cavity*
a *of Frog*
b *of Man*

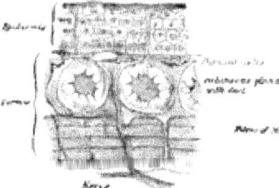

Fig 12 *Vertical section of skin*

W. & A.K. Johnston, Edinburgh & London

PLATE XXIV.

THE FROG—*continued.*

COMPARATIVE HISTOLOGY OF FROG AND MAN—*continued.*

Fig. 1. TRANSVERSE SECTION OF FROG'S FEMUR—

Periosteum (Gr. *peri*, around ; *osteon*, a bone), the investing sheath of connective tissue.
Osteoblast layer (Gr. *blastos*, a germ), connective-tissue corpuscles arranged in a layer.
Bone-cells derived from osteoblasts.
Concentric lamellæ of bony substance.

Figs. 2, 3, 4. TRANSVERSE AND LONGITUDINAL SECTIONS OF HARD COMPACT TISSUE OF HUMAN HUMERUS—

Haversian canals for blood-vessels to run through, seen branching in fig. 3.
Concentric lamellæ of bone round each Haversian canal.
Lacunæ (L. hollows), oval spaces containing bone-cells (fig. 4).
Canaliculi (L. little canals), very minute tubes connecting the lacunæ with one another.

Figs. 5, 6, 7. MUSCULAR TISSUE—

Fig. 5. *a, b.* STRIATED OR STRIPED MUSCLE OF FROG taken from thigh—

MUSCULAR FIBRE { Sarcolemma (Gr. *sarx*, flesh; *lemma*, a sheath), the enveloping structureless sheath (not shown).
Fibrillæ, the fibrils composing the fibre.
Nuclei, brought out by acetic acid.

Fig. 6. STRIPED HUMAN MUSCLE—

Fibres dividing longitudinally into fibrillæ and transversely into disks.

Fig. 7. SMOOTH OR UNSTRIPED MUSCULAR FIBRES FROM HUMAN ARTERIES—

Individual fibre-cells with elongated nucleus.

Figs. 8, 9. NERVOUS TISSUE—

Fig. 8. *a, b.* NERVE-FIBRES—

NERVE-FIBRE . { Primitive sheath, the investing structureless membrane.
Medullary sheath or white substance of Schwann.
Axis-cylinder, the central part, fibrillated at origin and termination.

Fig. 9. NERVE-CELLS—

Granular protoplasm, nucleus and nucleolus.
Processes or poles sometimes branched and continuous with axis cylinders of nerve-fibres.

Fig. 10. LIVER—

Hepatic or liver cells with nuclei.
Blood-capillaries in section, from the blood of which the cells secrete or strain off the bile.
Bile-capillaries, minute passages shown as swellings between the cells.

Fig. 11. EPIDERMIS OF FROG, surface view.

Fig. 12. VERTICAL SECTION OF SKIN OF FROG—

EPIDERMIS . . . Cells flattened and hardened towards the surface, plump and soft deeper down where produced.

DERMIS OR TRUE SKIN { Connective tissue, both varieties (Pl. XXIII. fig. 6).
Pigment-cells = connective-tissue corpuscles containing pigment.
Cutaneous glands, flask-shaped, lined by epidermis, and opening on the surface.

Fig. 13. NERVOUS AND CONNECTIVE ELEMENTS OF RETINA OF FROG—

CONNECTIVE . . { Connective tissue holding the nervous elements together, and extending from external limiting membrane at the base of the rods and cones to internal limiting membrane in contact with vitreous humour.
Fibres of Müller, probably connecting the two limiting membranes.

NERVOUS . . Rod and cone layer projecting beyond connective tissue, and embedded in choroid.

Fig. 14. EPITHELIUM FROM NASAL CHAMBER—

Epithelial cells, columnar, with outer ends broad and inner ends constricted and branched.
Olfactory cells, between epithelial cells, with fine hairs (Hiogr or small rods (Many), an outer fine process, and inner probably coming into connection with olfactory nerve, hence the name.

www.ingramcontent.com/pod-product-compliance
Lightning Source LLC
Chambersburg PA
CBHW030545270326
41927CB00008B/1519